IMAGES
*of America*

# OLD TORRANCE
## OLMSTED DISTRICTS

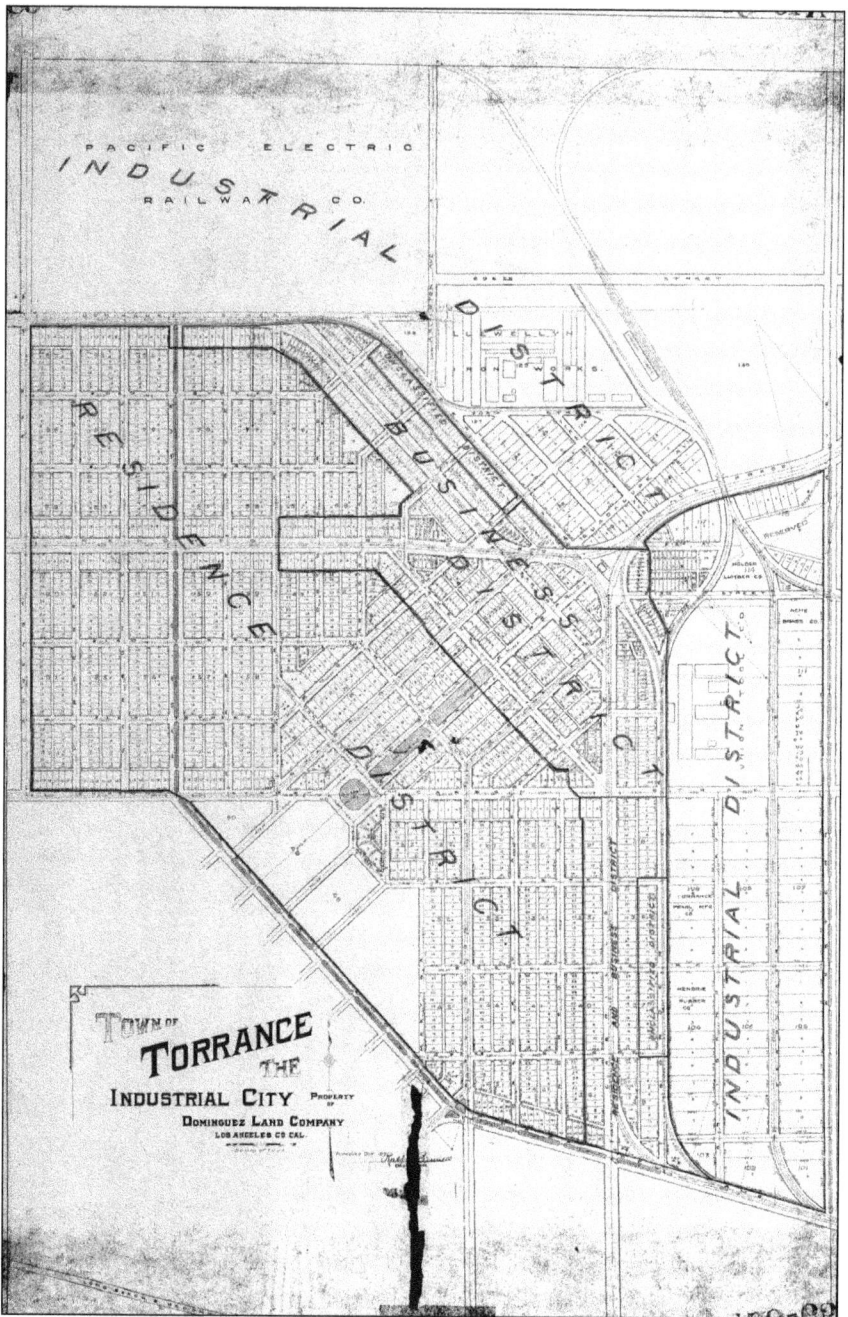

This is a copy of the layout for Torrance, California. A larger version is housed at the Torrance Historical Society and Museum. (Courtesy City of Torrance.)

ON THE COVER: Exactly as both Jared S. Torrance and Frederick Law Olmsted Jr. envisioned, these unidentified mothers and their children are enjoying the excellent climate and beautifully landscaped open space at Torrance Park. (Courtesy University of Southern California Regional History collection.)

IMAGES
*of America*

# OLD TORRANCE
## OLMSTED DISTRICTS

Bonnie Mae Barnard and
Save Historic Old Torrance

ARCADIA
PUBLISHING

Published by Arcadia Publishing
Charleston, South Carolina

Library of Congress Catalog Card Number: 2005930094

For all general information contact Arcadia Publishing at:
Telephone 843-853-2070
Fax 843-853-0044
E-mail sales@arcadiapublishing.com
For customer service and orders:
Toll-Free 1-888-313-2665

Visit us on the Internet at www.arcadiapublishing.com

# CONTENTS

# ACKNOWLEDGMENTS

No major accomplishment happens as the result of one person. This is true of the city of Torrance and of the writing and compiling of this book. Like the creation of the city of Torrance, this book was done with the help and cooperation of many people. Putting it together took many "Torranceonians" who love the vision-come-true that is *Old Torrance: Olmsted Districts*. Implicitly important are my husband, Don Barnard, and Mary Steinkamp. Because he loves me and this city, Don spent hundreds of hours scanning photographs and documents, numbering and renumbering them for this book, and reassuring me throughout the entire process. Mary volunteered her time to search high and low for sources of information for me. Without her help, years instead of months would have been involved in the research for this book. Mary also skillfully critiqued the drafts through the revision process.

Next I owe a debt of gratitude to those who serve on the executive board of Save Historic Old Torrance, The Olmsted District Preservation Association: Sara Guyan, Brenda Kulp, Nina McCoy, Ramie McCoy, Judith Weber, and Don and Mary. These great people not only provided me with their photographs and memories, but asked everyone with whom they came in contact for contributions. Without their help, I could not have accumulated well over 300 photographs from which to choose.

The people of Torrance are a community, and it is to the community I say "Thank you." Although not all of the photographs are from within Old Torrance, they are representative of the people, the times, and the area. Thank you for your photographs, your memories, and your interest in preserving the architectural charm and beauty of the original city of Torrance, designed by Frederick Law Olmsted Jr. of the Olmsted Brothers firm. Thank you to Frederick Law Olmsted Sr. for bequeathing his love of open space and natural beauty to his sons. Thank you to John Charles Olmsted and Frederick Law Olmsted Jr. for continuing to create landscapes by following that philosophy. Thank you to Jared Sidney Torrance for his vision of a modern industrial city, a garden city where people would be proud to work, live, and play. Thank you to Irving J. Gill, California's Modernist architect, and to Mr. Sinclair of the Dominguez Land Company for hiring Gill. Gill designed our graceful, simply elegant bridge, some of our business structures, and our modern homes. Thank you to the architects and builders whose craftsmanship is exhibited in the wonderfully diverse homes that comprise this charming original area of the city. Thank you to the people of Torrance who treasure their homes, yards, and neighborhoods. They continue to make Old Torrance a community where neighbors still greet each other on the sidewalk, sit on front porches, and where children play across several adjoining front yards. It is still a great place to live, work, and play. To all of you, I extend my sincerest and deepest thanks.

# INTRODUCTION

Today, as it was long ago, a portion of the story of the city of Torrance, California, is revealed in the names of its streets. Many are literally imprinted in the cement curbs of the streets. The predominant name in the area that became Old Torrance was Dominguez, reflecting the family who became the recipient of an 18th century land grant. The original northerly boundary of the city was Dominguez Way, honoring that 1784 Spanish land grant to Juan Jose Dominguez.

Thirteen years after Dominguez's death, the land grant was reconfirmed and officially passed to a nephew, Cristobal Dominguez. His son, Manuel, the next executor of the family estate, was commemorated by Manuel Avenue. Manuel Dominguez married Maria Engracia Cota in 1827, and her name is immortalized in two of our streets—Engracia and Cota Avenues in the heart of the original city.

Manuel and Maria Engracia Cota de Dominguez died within six months of each other, leaving the land to the couple's six surviving daughters: Ana Josefa, Guadalupe, Maria Dolores, Maria Victoria, Maria Susana, and Maria Jesus de los Reyes. Although Guadalupe's name still is visible in the cement of an Old Torrance street corner, the street name was changed to Post Avenue in honor of Judge George Post, the founder of Torrance National Bank, the first bank in the town.

The death of a Dominguez sister in 1907 paved the way for the city of Torrance to exist. Ana Josefa Dominguez de Guyer passed on, leaving her share of the estate equally to her five sisters. The Dominguez sisters in turn formed a corporation in 1910 representing the Guyer estate. This firm, the Dominguez Estate Company, soon held half of the original Dominguez land grant as a result of additional land deeded or sold to the company by the sisters. However, three of the married Dominguez daughters—Victoria, Dolores, and Susana—each formed separate companies to manage their estates. These were the Carson Estate Company, the Watson Land Company, and the Del Amo Estate Company. Those company names became names of our streets—Carson Street, Del Amo Boulevard, Plaza Del Amo, and Watson Street. Soon after the Dominguez Estate Company was formed, land sales began.

Those instrumental in the land purchases that became the original city of Torrance are also immortalized in our streets. A major thoroughfare, Redondo Boulevard, became Torrance Boulevard, named after Jared Sidney Torrance, president of the Dominguez Land Company. Stockholders of that land company included Merris Hellman, Joseph F. Sartori, John S. Cravens, and Dr. W. Jarvis Barlow, as well as Jared S. Torrance, who represented J. H. Adams and Company. They purchased 2,792 acres at $350 per acre from the Dominguez Estate Company and 730 acres from the Del Amo Estate Company for the creation of the would-be town. Two of those stockholders were immortalized in the names of Sartori and Cravens Avenues.

The city of Torrance was the brainchild of Jared Sidney Torrance. Originally from New York, Torrance was a resident of Pasadena and an extremely successful businessman. The city he envisioned for this ideally located town-to-be would not just be a single company town, but a town that offered its residents a variety of occupational and housing choices. It would have several major industrial factories that would provide ample employment. It would have a variety of home designs from which the employed man could choose. It would provide pleasant surroundings both at work and home, thereby providing employers with contented employees and the employees with a real community.

Another major aspect of Mr. Torrance's vision included home ownership. He believed that the working man who was happy at work and who owned his own home, would stay and contribute to the community. His vision was a city in which people were happy to work, live, and play. The industries, businesses, and residences of this community would be supplemented by a library, schools, hospital, and opportunities for cultural experiences. Perhaps Mr. Torrance's vision is best stated by Frederick Law Olmsted Jr. as he reiterated his understanding of said vision in a letter to Mr. Torrance:

> This company [Dominguez Land Company] intends to make its profit through creating and marketing a first class line of goods in the way of industrial sites, dwelling places for those engaged in the industries, and various incidentals through furnishing these goods of a quality that will make them worth more to the buyers and occupants, per dollar of cost, than any that can elsewhere be obtained . . . with a sufficiency of capital available it is a good business enterprise and will clearly work out to the great advantage of the resulting community.

To bring his vision into a workable plan would require big names and big bucks. Five years after the 1912 founding of the city, Torrance presented a glowing report on the city to the Torrance Chamber of Commerce. On February 16, 1917, he stated, "We employed the most eminent landscape architect. The complete plans cost $10,000." That landscape architect and city designer was Frederick Law Olmsted Jr.

The *Los Angeles Times* displayed a picture of the prominent Olmsted and proclaimed on December 22, 1911, "Huge Fee for Laying out Industrial City: Landscape Architect of International Reputation Here to Draw Plans for Great Dominguez Project." The *Los Angeles Examiner* announced on December 10, 1911, that "no meager, insufficient talent is to be employed in the project for a model industrial village on the Dominguez Ranch." This famous architect/planner was the progeny of Frederick Law Olmsted, the famed 19th-century architect and designer of New York City's Central Park; the park system of Buffalo, New York; San Francisco Public Grounds; Mount Royal Park, Montreal, Canada; and the U.S. Capitol Grounds, as well as the National Zoological Park, in Washington, D.C. The father had famously passed on to the son the philosophy of cooperation with nature to produce a calming, soothing feeling to be enjoyed by all who view a landscape design.

Olmsted Jr. carried the ideals of his father and mentor to new heights as the most accomplished landscape architect and city planner in the country. He created planning reports for growth and expansion for the suburbia of Newport, Rhode Island; Detroit, Michigan; Utica, New York; Boulder, Colorado; Pittsburgh, Pennsylvania, and Rochester, New York. Olmsted Jr. served two terms as president of the American Society of Landscape Architects and was a major author of the McMillan Plan, the comprehensive blueprint for transforming the nucleus of Washington, D.C., into further development of the nation's capital. He was appointed by President Taft to the then newly formed Fine Arts Commission, which provided supervising authority in aesthetic, architectural, and planning matters in the nation's capital. He taught architecture at Harvard University and created the Harvard curriculum for landscape architects and city planners. In 1909, he was selected as the president of the first National Conference on City Planning and the Problems of Congestion in Washington, D.C.

Olmsted's design is as easily distinguishable today as it was almost 100 years ago, when the city of Torrance began. His trademark, the inclusion of nature, is evident on the street named El Prado, which translates to "the Meadow." It is a serene parkway with open space and trees and a spectacular view from Torrance High School, its highest point. From this vista on a clear day, one could view Mount San Antonio, commonly referred to as Mount Baldy. The beautiful expanse of El Prado was designed to join the city's Residential District and the Business District by a vista of nature.

Another trademark of Olmsted's design is evident in the original city of Torrance's districting, in which consideration was allotted for industry, business, residences, and growth of any of those. Each district was designed to make the working and living environments pleasant to the inhabitants. With the California climate in mind, Olmsted positioned the Industrial District to take full advantage of the faithful Pacific Ocean breezes that have usually greeted the city each afternoon. In Torrance's formative years, those breezes sent smoke and pollutants away from the residents. The Business District was designed to be within walking distance of the eastern end of the spectacularly tree-lined El Prado—the center of the Residential District.

Olmsted's street designs allowed views of roads not taken, breaks from linear vistas, and are still easily seen in Old Torrance. He designed curved streets and a roundabout at the pinnacle of El Prado, where Torrance High School is now located. Sadly the roundabout was removed. Nevertheless the streets of Old Torrance definitely reflect the Olmsted design.

The second big name brought in to bring Torrance's vision and Olmsted's plan into fruition was the Modernist Irving J. Gill, the would-be-city's resident architect. La Jolla boasts the largest collection of structures in California designed by Gill, but Torrance appears to have the second largest collection. Gill designed the railroad bridge whose graceful arches are a thing of function and beauty, marking the eastern entrance to Old Torrance. Gill's works include the impressive and compellingly designed depot, which was utilized by the Pacific Electric Railway; the tract office of Thomas D. Campbell, which would become the Torrance National Bank; the Murray, Roi Tan, and Brighton Hotels and office buildings with sophisticatedly simple lines; and 10 small, Modernistic concrete homes. The bridge's arches are now accented with lush foliage, as Gill planned, and continue to add that powerful, majestic sense to the eastern gateway of the city.

This book is designed as windows on the past, a tour through Old Torrance as it existed in the first half of the 20th century. At that time, Torrance was a model industrial city like no other, the realized vision of both Jared Sidney Torrance and Frederick Law Olmsted Jr.—a truly novel and visionary place for people to live, work, and play.

"It is not enough to build modern factory buildings," declared Jared Sidney Torrance on October 27, 1912. "The time has come when we must go beyond this and see that the man at work, the man who really makes the factory possible, has ideal living conditions. . . . It is mental as well as physical health that must be offered him." Jared Sidney Torrance, pictured here in 1906, is the city of Torrance's namesake. (Courtesy Gowanda Area Historical Society.)

"It is the comprehensive master plan . . . that is the key to ensuring 'harmonious, beautiful and convenient residential communities,'" professed Frederick Law Olmsted Jr., the designer of the city of Torrance, as quoted in *A Modern Arcadia* by Susan L. Klaus. With plans in hand, Frederick Law Olmsted Jr. is pictured in 1910. (Courtesy National Park Service, Frederick Law Olmsted National Historic Site.)

"If we, the architects of the West, wish to do great and lasting work, we must dare to be simple . . . and get back to the source of all architectural strength—the straight line, the arch, the cube and the circle," Irving J. Gill proclaimed in his 1916 *The Craftsman* magazine article, "The Home of the Future." Irving J. Gill, Modernist and resident architect for the forming city of Torrance, is seen here in 1913. (Courtesy and copyright © San Diego Historical Society.)

# One

# THE INDUSTRIAL DISTRICT
## A PLACE TO WORK

This free ticket provided a visit to the "Beauty Spot of Southern California: The Industrial City Torrance!" In 1912, a trip included a snack known as a "Dainty Lunch" and a free ride to entice people and businesses to relocate to Torrance. (Courtesy Doris Greene.)

Passengers boarded trains at the Dominguez Tower. Here Long Beach Flyer No. 363 arrives at Dominguez Junction, commemorating the Dominguez family, which was so influential in Torrance and greater South Bay affairs. (Courtesy Los Angeles Railroad Heritage Foundation, www.larhf.org.)

All aboard! The Pacific Electric 1057 bound for Torrance arrived in 1939. (Courtesy Los Angeles Railroad Heritage Foundation, www.larhf.org.)

In this expanse, note the Pacific Electric Freighter No. 1631 heading into Torrance. The Pacific Electric lines assured easy shipment of raw materials needed for the Industrial District of Torrance, as well as the rapid shipment of manufactured items from Torrance. (Courtesy Los Angeles Railroad Heritage Foundation, www.larhf.org.)

TORRANCE BLVD. Looking West 1921

A03

This impressive bridge was designed by Modernist architect Irving J. Gill. This 1912 glimpse shows the flat upper surface of the bridge upon which the Pacific Electric trains traveled, as well as the interior arches where the Pacific Electric Red Cars passed and the exterior arches through which the residents drove. (Courtesy Doris Greene.)

The Union Tool Company. Torrance, California.

The Industrial District included the Union Tool Company (UTCO), which was constructed in 1913 on 25 acres. Important buildings are the main shop; the forge shop, which was touted as the most modern and up-to-date forge plant in the United States; the power plant, the most modern steam plant on the coast; the engine room; the warehouse; the foundry; eight miles of industrial tracks with a standard-gauge, 40-ton locomotive and steam crane hoist; and the administration building. UTCO provided a West Coast novelty: sanitation, including wash rooms with toilets, sinks, and showers, according to the May 1, 1921, edition of the *Los Angeles Times*.

·The UTCO News·

Vol. 2                    No. 2

PUBLISHED MONTHLY
DEVOTED TO THE INTERESTS OF AND EDITED BY
The Union Tool Company Employees

JUNE 1921

Here is a copy of the *UTCO News*, the newsletter created by the Union Tool Company employees—
1,200 men and women in an almost fraternal society, under the spirit of teamwork. This ideal
was designed to be maintained in the spirit of the broadest possible cooperation by the entire
personnel, from laborer to president. (Courtesy Sara and Ellen Guyan.)

15

A look inside the Pacific Electric Railway Shops, located in the Industrial District, revealed the men who repaired and maintained the Red Cars at work. (Courtesy Doris Greene.)

UTCO became the National Supply Company, and this 1950s aerial view shows all of the buildings that were formerly Union Tool Company. Like its predecessor, National—as the locals called it—was a great company for which to work. It is not uncommon for several members of a family to be employed by National. (Courtesy Alison Jones.)

This is a closer look at the National Supply Company's main entrance. (Courtesy Alison Jones.)

Blanche Nagy certainly offered some perspective. These giant barrels forged by the forge crew are jackets for Byron Jackson's famous pumps. They weighed 22,000 pounds each and measured 92 inches long and 39 inches in diameter at the large end, and 35 inches in diameter at the small end. (Courtesy Alison Jones.)

Another perspective was provided by Gordon Jones as he stood inside this giant forged piece. (Courtesy Alison Jones.)

Supervisor Gordon Jones of the National Supply Company is shown working at his desk. Notice the ink bottle in his open desk drawer and, under the glass of his desk, the photographs of his daughter Alison and son Gordie. Gordon Jones worked at National for 32 years. (Courtesy Alison Jones.)

In 1920, employees gather near the forge of National Supply Company. From left, the 12th man in the second row is John Guyan. (Courtesy Sara and Ellen Guyan.)

In the 1930s, friendly steel foundry workers gather at National Supply. John W. Guyan is in the second row. (Courtesy Sara and Ellen Guyan.)

National Supply Company employees gathered to offer best wishes to the unidentified retiree. Directly behind the man of that particular hour is John W. Guyan. (Courtesy Sara and Ellen Guyan.)

Hendrie Rubber Company and Glass Factory, Torrance, California.

The W. C. Hendrie Rubber Company was the first and largest of its kind in Southern California. The company's large steel and concrete structure was built at a cost of $100,000, housed $80,000 worth of equipment, and was supplied with $20,000 in raw rubber before it opened in Torrance on August 16, 1913. The plant supplied 14,600 tires and 14,000 inner tubes annually. The forward-thinking company then anticipated an output capacity of 100,000 tires per day, according to the August 15, 1913, edition of the *Los Angeles Times*.

1307:—Hendrie Tire Plant, Torrance, Calif.

1314:—Torrance Window Glass Factory, Torrance, Calif.

The Hurrie Window Glass Factory was built in 1916. The opening of this factory prompted the Dominguez Land Company to hire C. A. Crews of Pasadena to build an additional 50 bungalows along Cabrillo and Andreo Avenues in order to provide housing for the 100 or more employees that Hurrie would need. The original plant experienced a fire, which destroyed the building on July 27, 1919. However, a new plant was constructed within 90 days. It is believed that this is the new plant.

Llewellyn Iron Works and American System of Reinforcing, Torrance, California. 1921

Adjacent to Hurrie Window Glass Factory were the vast buildings and acreage of Llewellyn Iron Works—known as "The American System of Reinforcement," which occupied 25 acres in Torrance. Llewellyn Iron Works produced the largest amount of hearth steel and products on the Pacific Coast and employed 600 workers in 1921, with plans for expansion and more employment. (Courtesy Doris Greene.)

This westward view takes in the marvelous bridge designed by Modernist architect Irving Gill. Here, in 1963, it is draped with adorning foliage, adding to the beauty of its graceful lines. (Courtesy Doris Greene.)

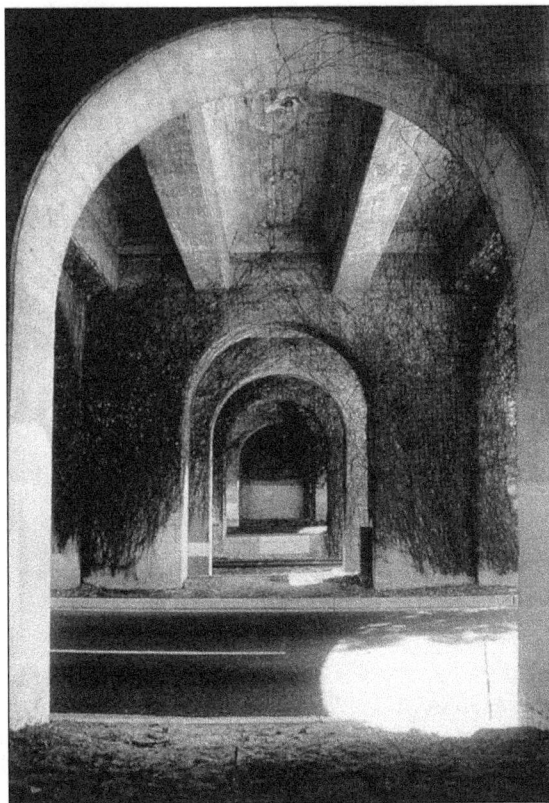

This rare view under the arches of Gill's bridge demonstrates the amazing ingenuity and magnificent simplicity of his design. The underpass is graced with foliage. (Courtesy Thomas Hines.)

Another Irving Gill design of which the City of Torrance proudly boasts is the extraordinary depot. Designed as a thing of function and beauty, with its stately dome, arched parapet, and regal colonnade, the depot served the Pacific Electric Railway and today remains as a reminder of the Red Cars' heyday. Just as the secretary of the interior recommends that historic buildings be preserved and used for new functions, the Depot Restaurant is now the site of the fine dining creations of Chef Michael Shafer. (Courtesy Doris Greene.)

Near the depot was the Thomas D. Campbell Tract Office building. Note the bicycle and motorcar parked in front. In 1912, Campbell's office was in charge of the promotion and sale of real estate for the new town of Torrance. The building itself, with a parapet at each end, as well as the large building behind it, are Irving Gill designs. The following year, the smaller building served as Judge George Post's First National Bank of Torrance.

# Two

# THE BUSINESS DISTRICT
## A PLACE OF COMMERCE

The Business District became the hub of commerce for the people of Torrance. Note that the buildings are designed to have storefronts on the lower levels and provide apartments on the upper levels. Irving Gill's depot is at the far end of the street. (Courtesy Doris Greene.)

The inside of Paige's Grocery store, located on El Prado Avenue, is seen here selling the hot item of the day—Royal Baking Powder (foreground). It was touted as requiring fewer eggs than other baking powder. (Courtesy Doris Greene.)

Sartori Avenue was lined with ornate streetlights and the more "modern" motorcars. On the left corner, with the clock, is the Torrance First National Bank. On the opposite corner, notice the Edison Company building. Downtown Torrance bustled with business. (Courtesy Doris Greene.)

This is payday, some time in 1929, and checks are being cashed by the First National Bank. Talk about a long line! Most of the customers are factory workers in the Industrial District, but the Business District workers are easily spotted, distinguishable by attire. Thirty-one factories existed in the city of Torrance in 1929, and the weekly deposits by the local employees of the city totaled nearly $1.5 million per week. The clerk in the foreground was Edward C. Nelson. (Courtesy University of Southern California Regional History collection.)

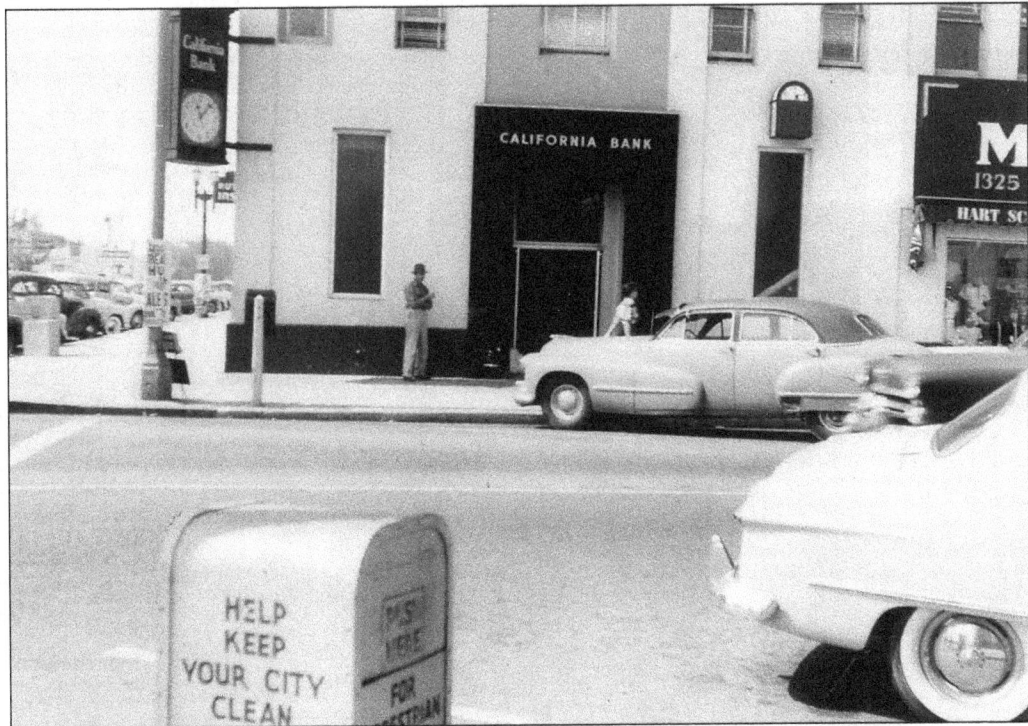

Outside the bank, the same clock ticked in the 1950s as it did in bygone decades, but notice that the exterior reflected a change to California Bank. A glance at the windows above revealed that the upper story became a professional level. Local dentist Dr. R. E. Jackson had his office there. (Courtesy Phyllis Post.)

This historic brick building still stands in the downtown of Old Torrance—the Business District. On the lower level is Sam Levy Clothing and Shoes. Levy and his family provided the residents of Torrance with the earliest and longest-running business in the district. One local story about Levy reports that when he purchased his building, the agent insisted that he also purchase earthquake insurance, much to Levy's displeasure. However, in 1933, Sam discovered the wisdom in that purchase after the Long Beach earthquake, in which many businesses experienced damage. Levy was the only business owner who had purchased such insurance. (Courtesy Alan Schwartz.)

How about a pair of shoes? Inside the Levy building, Florsheim shoes were stored in abundance and friendly gentlemen waited to assist the footwear customer. The walls were lined with boxes of shoes. (Courtesy Alan Schwartz.)

28

A southward look on Sartori Avenue during the 1930s brought the Torrance Theatre, left, into view. On the right was the beautiful building of the Bank of America, as well as diagonally parked motorcars. (Courtesy Alan Schwartz.)

SARTORI AVENUE at MARCELINA – 1936

In 1936, the theater's marquee invited patrons inside to the double feature—*The Ex-Mrs. Bradford* starring Jean Arthur and William Powell and "*Everybody's Old Man*—for just a few cents. To the left of the theater is a banner advertising the Kelvinator, the newest refrigerator. (Courtesy Doris Greene.)

Across the street from the theater was this ornate building, which housed the Bank of Italy before it became the Bank of America. In addition to the artistic design on the front and the regal, rectangular columns, notice the colonnade down the sides. Even the name of the bank on both the side and the front is in keeping with the architecture of the building. (Courtesy Alan Schwartz.)

The elegant Bank of America building's clock says 3:10 p.m., and the bank is closed. An ornate crown molding separates the wall and ceiling, and the ceiling lights and the turrets atop each teller window depict banking in bygone decades. (Courtesy Alan Schwartz.)

Two 1947 pay warrants typical of their era—one dated June 5 and the other October 3—were deposited in the Bank of America. Both are from the City of Torrance to Sam Levy and signed by the mayor, city treasurer, and city clerk. (Courtesy Alan Schwartz.)

In 1934, a Torrance Ice Company truck is parked in front of a gas station. The truck brought the ice needed for the new convenience of ice boxes. They quickly became much more popular than the cooler shelves of home cabinets. (Courtesy Doris Greene.)

A consistent sight in 1929 was the venerable King's Nursery truck, with its wood-spoked wheels and convertible cab. It delivered shrubs, trees, and other nursery items to Torrance residents. John R. King offered a friendly smile as he went by. (Courtesy Doris Greene.)

Longtime residents recall that it was often tempting to stop on Cravens Avenue, as this bicyclist has, to purchase a delectable soft-serve treat from the third oldest Fosters Freeze building in Los Angeles County. Part of the first franchise business in Southern California, this Fosters Freeze, located at 1609 Cravens Avenue, was a typical stop after a movie at the theater diagonally across the street, and a local place for young and old alike. Constructed in 1947, it opened in 1948 and continues through publication date to serve the same desserts to Torrance residents and visitors that is has for 57 years. This Fosters Freeze has provided, and continues to provide, a "first job" to many of Torrance's young residents. (Courtesy Barnard collection.)

FIREHOUSE, POLICE STATION, CITY HALL, JAIL   TORRANCE, CA   1923

In 1929, these rather official-looking public servants were the members of the Torrance Fire Department. The firemen are seen here with their car and truck in front of the building which served as the firehouse, police station, city hall, and jail in the growing city of Torrance. (Courtesy Doris Greene.)

Designed by Walker and Eisen, the regal Torrance City Hall Building located on Cravens Avenue proudly served residents for several generations before becoming a local cable company facility. (Courtesy University of Southern California Regional History collection.)

At the corner of Cravens Avenue and Marcelina Street was Harvel's, the local automotive service center. The Bell telephone signs drew attention to the phone booth located outside of Harvel's. This business provided many first-time jobs to the local teens. (Courtesy Alan Schwartz collection.)

Looking from the phone booth toward the street, this young Harvel's attendant was providing the service that came with any purchase of gasoline. Notice that the pump clearly states that the gasoline contains lead. (Courtesy Doris Greene.)

Since 1936, this stately U.S. post office building has operated on Marcelina Street. (Courtesy Alan Schwartz.)

The Mayfair Creamery, located at 1326 Post Avenue, is pictured here in 1937. The creamery had several trucks delivering milk in glass bottles to the people of Torrance. In 1932, it advertised in the *Torch*, the Torrance High School Yearbook, that its milk "will build a strong, healthy body as you will build a core of knowledge." As if it needed to, the advertised also declared that "It's good." Many a Torranceonian agreed. (Courtesy Doris Greene.)

PUBLIC LIBRARY  TORRANCE, CA  Post avenue at Cravens 1936

So important was it to J. S. Torrance that the residents of the city of Torrance have access to a library, that he donated 300 books to his cousin Isabel Henderson, who opened the town's first library in her home, located at 1804 Gramercy Avenue. This structure, located at 1345 Post Avenue, is a Walker and Eisen design and the city's first "official" library building. Today the building is the proud home of the Torrance Historical Society Museum, which houses mementos and memorabilia of the city's early days.

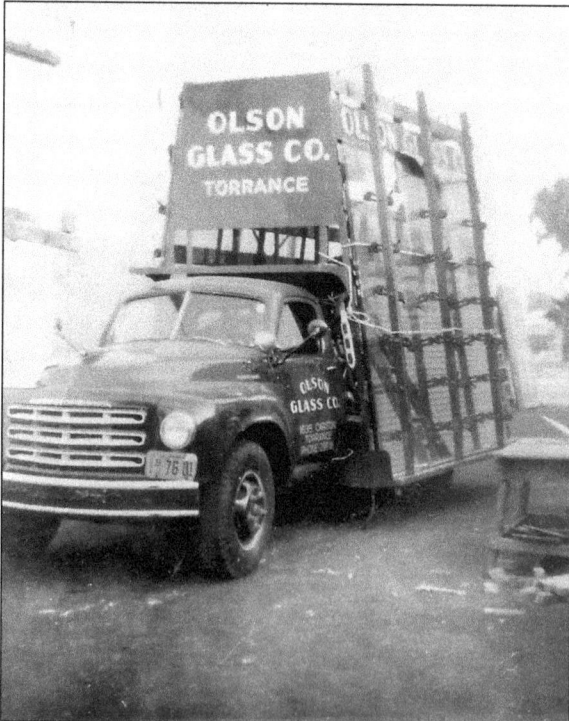

In the early decades of the 20th century, trucks became an important tool for getting products to residents. The Olson Glass Company of Torrance delivered to companies and residents alike. (Courtesy Doris Greene.)

At 1230 Cravens Avenue was another impressive building—Stone and Myers Mortuary and its Chapel of the Bells. The mortuary advertised in the 1932 edition of *Torch*, the Torrance High School Yearbook, with only three words: Stone and Myers. One signer, known decades later only as Louise, added rather ominously in Alice Hammond's yearbook . . . "will get you yet." Today this building has found an excellent reuse. It is the home of the Volunteer Center for the South Bay, which connects volunteers with organizations. Stone and Myers moved into a building across the street, so the caption added by Louise still may be correct. (Courtesy Doris Greene.)

Looking north on Cabrillo Avenue, the center of the street made way for the Pacific Electric Railway Red Cars. The building to the left, the Brighton Hotel, was designed by Modernist architect Irving Gill. This building still graces the corner of Cabrillo Avenue and Carson Street and the lower level still serves as a business location while the upper units serve as apartments.

Looking south on Cabrillo Avenue, Howard's Jewelers and the Ed Schwartz Building business are visible. (Courtesy Alan Schwartz.)

This is the same street corner as above and the same Howard's Jewelers—only in the aftermath of the 1933 Long Beach earthquake, which was actually centered in Compton and killed 120 people. Residents gathered to see firsthand the damage to their community. (Courtesy Phyllis Post.)

On Carson Street, a peek inside Brown Shoe Repair showed Garland Brown, the owner, at the counter. Garland completed a second-grade education in Missouri and worked both for a railroad and hog ranch before coming with his young bride to Torrance, where he established this shoe repair shop. His employees worked at some of the many treadle sewing machines used in shoe repair. An employee's child naps on the couch in the foreground. (Courtesy Gail Kaopua.)

Also on Carson Street, Fred Hansen Jr. manned his family's Texaco gas station in 1942. During World War II, the Hansens had difficulty obtaining tires and batteries to sell because industry became geared to provide for the needs of the military and supplies for civilians were rationed. Before Pearl Harbor, gasoline was 15¢ per gallon, but it reached 18¢ during the war. Only three gallons were allowed to be pumped per customer, except for doctors, who were allowed five gallons.

In 1933, Fred Hansen Sr. purchased this Texaco gas station, located at the corner of Carson Street and Arlington Avenue. The Hansens lived directly across the street at 2063 Carson Street. Fred Hansen Jr. frequently sat on the porch steps of the house waiting for customers. When one arrived, he ran across the street to provide service. On the first day of business in 1933, gasoline was 12 gallons for $1 and Hansen's sales for the day totaled $6.32.

Since the Hansens lived across the street at 2063 Carson Street, it was easy to see how they had quick access to their Texaco gas station. With his home, real estate office, and gas station all within a quick walk, Hansen lived out J. S. Torrance's ideal of the city as a place to live, work, and play.

# *Three*

# THE RESIDENTIAL DISTRICT
## HOSPITAL AND HOUSES

1309:—Looking North on Carson St., Torrance, Calif.

Looking down Carson Street in the 1920s meant a view of oil derricks much taller than the trees. There were many more wooden derricks than motorcars in the young town of Torrance. (Courtesy Doris Greene.)

The Torrance Health Center is pictured in the 1940s on Carson Street. In the second row is John R. Guyan, the center's janitor. This building still stands today. (Courtesy Sara and Ellen Guyan.)

Part of the original plan for the City of Torrance was the building of a hospital—the Jared Sidney Torrance Memorial Hospital, located at 1425 Engracia Avenue in the Residential District. However, the founding father died in 1921 and never saw the completed hospital. His will left more than $10,000 for construction of the building. (Courtesy University of Southern California Regional History collection.)

This is the side and rear view of the Jared Sidney Torrance Memorial Hospital. After J. S. Torrance's death, Mrs. Torrance spent a great deal of time and energy making sure the hospital became a reality, which it did in 1924. During the Depression, Mrs. Torrance saw to it that the hospital had the necessary supplies. A wood-spoked motorcar has stopped across the street. (Courtesy University of Southern California Regional History collection.)

The entrance of the hospital included marvelous details above the door. Within the arch, the script reads, "Jared Sidney Torrance Memorial Hospital." The decorative carvings horizontally above the door feature cherubs, a Phoenix, and flowers. The door itself was multi-paned with ornately etched glass. (Courtesy Doris Greene.)

Within one year, not only had the landscaping around the Jared Sidney Torrance Memorial Hospital grown, but it served as the welcoming place to a growing population. The infants born in 1925—the first year the hospital provided services—are seen here with their mothers. Standing third from left is Blanche McVicar, holding her baby daughter Phyllis. Seated in the second seat from the left is Dorothy Post, with her baby son Jim. (Courtesy Phyllis Post.)

This 1960s view shows the Jared Sidney Torrance Memorial Hospital, with its carefully manicured landscape. (Courtesy Doris Greene.)

Jared Sidney Torrance Memorial Hospital
1425 Engracia Avenue, ∵ Standardized Class A Hospital ∵ Torrance, California

## Hospital Birth Certificate

This Certifies that _John Alexander Guyan_
was born in Jared Sidney Torrance Memorial Hospital of Torrance, California, on the

_16th_ day of _May_ A. D. 19_41_

In Witness Whereof the said Hospital has caused this Certificate to be signed by its duly authorized officer and its Corporate Seal to be hereunto affixed.

Hospital Number _19099_ _Winnie E. Wagner R.N._
Charge Nurse

Doctor _____ _Esther J. Maxwell, R.N._
Superintendent

A baby's new footprints bookend a picture of the hospital on the birth certificates from the Jared Sidney Torrance Hospital. This 1941 birth certificate states that the hospital is a Standardized Class A Hospital, a tribute both to Jared Sidney Torrance for his vision and generosity, and to his wife, Helena Torrance, whose involvement in the success of the hospital continued for the remainder of her life. (Courtesy Sara and Ellen Guyan.)

45

A home in Torrance, California, was easy to purchase through the Dominguez Land Company, as this June 1921 advertisement in the *UTCO News* purports. It explains how just a few dollars more a year will save the home buyer time and provide an $800 equity within one short year. (Courtesy of Sara and Ellen Guyan collection.)

Fred Hansen Sr. didn't purchase his home through the Dominguez Land Company. Instead he bought the land and he and his brother built the house. Total expenditures for the building of the house came to $3,700 in 1920 dollars. (Courtesy of Fred Hansen Jr.)

A well-known local doctor, Dr. Jesse Lancaster, resided at 1451 Post Avenue. This Craftsman-style structure has provided, and provides today, a lifetime of comfort with character. (Courtesy Phyllis Post.)

Seated on the running board of his parents' modern motorcar in 1919 is little George Lancaster, with his puppy. (Courtesy Phyllis Post.)

Also on Post Avenue is the large Spanish Revival home of Judge George W. Post, founder of the Torrance National Bank. This house is a marvelous Old Torrance landmark today. (Courtesy Phyllis Post.)

HOW THE JONESES LIVE IN TORRANCE

Talk about keeping up with the Joneses. This tree-lined street and adorable home is featured in a postcard labeled "How the Joneses live in Torrance," promoting home ownership and the comfortable life envisioned by the city's creators. (Courtesy Doris Greene.)

Looking north toward Carson Street on Andreo Avenue, the view throughout most of the 20th century has taken in the California Craftsman bungalows that line the street. These were some of the first homes built in the city; each home came with a fireplace. Catch sight of the tree branches blowing easterly on the left from Gramercy Avenue, the next street west of Andreo, and the industry to the far northeast. Because of the dependable Pacific Ocean breeze blowing eastward, Olmsted guaranteed that the smoke from the industry blew away from the residential areas.

Just two blocks west of Andreo Avenue were more Craftsman-style bungalows. Though small in this c. 1912 photograph, the trees indicate that Arlington Avenue was planned as a tree-lined street with alley access behind the home.

This charming wood-framed house at 1222 Arlington Avenue served as the Burger family's home until 1945, when daughter Alice Burger Hammond and her husband moved in. It is equally enchanting today. (Courtesy Alice Burger Hammond.)

Alice's parents had this house built in front of wood-framed house at 1222 Arlington Avenue in order to give the old family home to Alice and her new husband, who came home from military service in 1945. (Courtesy Alice Burger Hammond.)

50

The inviting porch of the Guyan residence at 2119 Gramercy Avenue provided additional living space and an excellent view of the neighborhood. Note the vented attic and the exposed eaves as well as the double-hung wooden windows. Although many California Craftsman bungalows were built in the town, they weren't at all a cookie-cutter design, as variety in this style abounds. (Courtesy Sara and Ellen Guyan.)

Parked in front of the house next to 2119 Gramercy Avenue in the 1950s is the large family station wagon. The variety of homes on the street can be seen in the background. In the distance, to the left of the telephone pole, is the water tower in the Industrial District. (Courtesy Sara and Ellen Guyan.)

At home, playing with her puppy in the yard at 2121 Gramercy Avenue, is 13-year-old Phyllis McVicar. (Courtesy Phyllis Post.)

Kern Court, Torrance, California.

This bungalow court is typical of the courts built to accommodate employees of the many industries in the city. Like other bungalow courts, Kern Court at 208th Street was not only a home to workers, but a miniature community with a social meeting place, such as a fountain. Most of the homes had one bedroom. This bungalow court is gone today, and only a few remain in the city of Torrance.

# Four

# The Residential District
## Churches and Families

The happy wedding day of Kathy and Keith Arnold took place at Nativity Catholic Church, located at 1447 Engracia Avenue, across from Triangle Park. Note the beauty of the interior of the building and the stained-glass windows. (Courtesy Brenda Kulp.)

The 1949 wedding of George and Phyllis Post took place at the Saint Andrew's Episcopal Church, across the street from the Jared Sidney Torrance Memorial Hospital. On this particular day, the nurses from the hospital came out to watch the wedding. The wedding reception also took place at the church. The guests were served cake, punch, and two different colored mints. (Courtesy Phyllis Post.)

Gordon and Virginia Jones's storybook
wedding, just after the end of World War II in
1945, took place at Saint Andrew's Episcopal
Church, located at 1432 Engracia Avenue.
(Courtesy Alison Jones collection.)

A local town hero's wedding also took place
in 1945. Louis Zamperini, pronounced dead
by the U.S. Air Force, returned home alive.
He met, and within a short time, married
his sweetheart, Cynthia Applewhite of
Miami Beach. Pictured, from left to right, are
Sylvia Zamperini Flammer; Harvey Flammer,
Sylvia's husband; Virginia Zamperini; the
newlyweds Cynthia and Louis Zamperini;
Pete Zamperini; Louise Zamperini and her
husband, Anthony Zamperini. Louis Zamperini's
best seller, *Devil at My Heels*, tells his amazing life
story as an Olympic athlete, wartime pilot, and
prisoner of war. (Courtesy Barnard collection.)

On September 13, 1906, Jean Mavor and John R. Guyan were married. In 1956, they celebrated their 50th wedding anniversary in Torrance, California. (Courtesy Sara and Ellen Guyan.)

In 1958, three generations of Guyans joined together for the bride's family photograph in front of the home at 1807 Andreo Avenue. Pictured, from left to right, are (first row) Rosemary Folts, bride Beverly Folts, and Jenny Guyan; (second row) Ethel Guyan Folts and Rosemary Guyan; (third row) Bob Folts, John R. Guyan, and Jean Guyan. (Courtesy Sara and Ellen Guyan.)

Alice Burger is seen as a vivacious Torrance High student sitting on the porch at her home on Cedar Avenue, before that particular street's name changed to Crenshaw Boulevard. (Courtesy Alice Burger Hammond.)

In 1934, Alice's boyfriend, Bill, is seen at her parents' home on Arlington Avenue. Beside Bill is his father, Mr. Berkert, and Alice's sister Jane Burger, wearing a stylish hat and two-piece suit. The Burgers, Joneses, Hansons, Zamperinis, and other families of Old Torrance's prewar and postwar days lived in a manner that evoked the realization of Jared Sidney Torrance's vision of a place to work, live, and play.

The Zamperini family is seen at dinner in their home at 2028 Gramercy Avenue. With four children of their own, the Zamperinis were frequent hosts. Seated at the dining room table, from left to right, are Louis Zamperini, Felice Cain, Gordon DeMond, Gwen DeMond, Anthony (Tony) Zamperini, Louise Zamperini, Virginia Zamperini, Pete Zamperini, and Clark Crane. Sylvia Zamperini took this photograph. The built-in hutch holds Mrs. Zamperini's china. (Courtesy Barnard collection.)

In 1949, Phyllis and George Post shared their first Christmas. Notice the double-hung wooden windows to the right of the tree. They are draped with sheer curtains, which reveal the circular pull for the window shade. (Courtesy Phyllis Post.)

Home and family life in 1945 Torrance were typified by the Zamperinis. Note the fashions and hairstyles of the World War II era, as well as the cabriole-legged couch and the rugs over the hardwood floors. Seated, from left to right, are Sylvia, Anthony (Tony), Louis (Louie), Pete, Louise, and Virginia. (Courtesy Barnard collection.)

What family hasn't taken a group picture on the front lawn? Seen here at Alonzo and Emma Burger's home at 1508 Acacia Avenue, the generations gather together. From left to right are (first row) Jane Burger, Alice Burger, Myrtle Falihee, Emma Burger, and Grace Olson; (second row) Henry Lintott (superintendent of U.S. Steel), Leslie Berger; Alonzo Burger, Lettie Lintott, and Tom Falihee. (Courtesy Alice Burger Hammond.)

A young family gathered on the front lawn at 2119 Gramercy Avenue for this 1943 photograph. Pictured, from left to right, are (first row) John Guyan, Billy Guyan, and Donald Guyan; (second row) John W. Guyan and Ellen Guyan. (Courtesy Sara and Ellen Guyan.)

The boys take the spotlight. In the background, all of the houses seem to be the same distance from the street and each lawn blends into the next, with only a walkway separating them. This expanse can still be seen not only on Gramercy Avenue, but on many of the streets in Old Torrance. Pictured, from left to right in this portrait of fledgling masculinity, are John, Billy, and Donald Guyan. (Courtesy Sara and Ellen Guyan.)

Here's Alice Burger again, this time holding the baby of her minister, Kemp Winkler, assisted by her neighborhood friend Joy Fossum. Young girls typically assisted with the care of younger children. (Courtesy Alice Burger Hammond.)

In 1945, the Zamperinis share a pleasant family meal. The tablecloth is the product of one year's on-and-off efforts by Louis Zamperini. Pictured, from left to right, are Louise, Pete, Louis, Anthony (Tony), Virginia, and Sylvia. The Zamperini name lives on in Torrance as the official name of the city's airport, Zamperini Field, and Zamperini Way, the street leading to the airport. (Courtesy Barnard collection.)

This happy group gathers at Jane and Leslie Burger's home in 1942, when family togetherness was especially appreciated during wartime. Pictured, from left to right, are Alice Burger, Kenneth Haslen, Harold "Skipper" Haslen, Jean Haslen, and Stan McElderry. (Courtesy Alice Burger Hammond.)

Three years later, in 1945, the same family gathers in front of the same house. This time, the grandparents, Jane and Leslie Burger (center), join in the picture. Pictured, from left to right, are (first row) Harold "Skipper" Haslem; (second row) Kenneth Haslem, Jean Haslem, Jane Burger, Leslie Burger, Stan McElderry, and Alice Burger. (Courtesy Alice Burger Hammond.)

## Five

# THE RESIDENTIAL DISTRICT
## HEROES AND HOME

In 1932, Freddie Hansen Jr. proudly poses in his newly purchased Boy Scouts of America uniform. His sister Louise stands beside him. (Courtesy Fred Hansen Jr.)

Local heroes, Boy Scout Troop No. 217, No. 218, and No. 219, pose in 1933 in front of the Torrance High School Auditorium. Bob Llewellyn was scoutmaster. Troop No. 218 was the Drum and Bugle Corps that played at night for the community. Identified in the second row, fifth and sixth from the left, are Fred Hansen Jr. and Bill Keffer. The entire back row, from left to right, consisted of Eagle Scouts Carl Paxman, unidentified, unidentified, James Miller, George Bradford, and unidentified. The auditorium was severely damaged by the 1933 Long Beach earthquake, which caused its complete demolishment. (Courtesy Fred Hansen Jr.)

66

Two of the Boy Scouts of America Troop No. 219 were Eagle Scouts and good friends—Phil Hoffman and George "Sunny" Post. (Courtesy Phyllis Post.)

Home on leave, this unidentified U.S. Army soldier spends some time with his sweetheart in Old Torrance. (Courtesy Alison Jones.)

The biggest local hero, Louis Zamperini, was given the nickname the "Torrance Tornado" by reporters. Louis broke the mile record in track at Torrance High School. In this photograph, he is seen breaking his own mile record as a University of Southern California Trojan. The Torrance Tornado represented the United States in the 1936 Olympic games in Berlin. (Courtesy Barnard collection.)

In 1942, a couple of soldiers, George Post, left, and Phil Hoffman, are home on leave, visiting their old hangout, Harvel's garage. Harvel's was the place where thehigh-school boys worked, meaning it was also frequented by the high school girls. Despite what anyone said, the girls didn't go to Harvel's to check out the tires or crankcases. (Courtesy Phyllis Post collection.)

This young pilot is packing a string of ammunition as long as he is tall for another ascent into the skies. Smiling in front of his aircraft is "Sunny" Post (George Post). (Courtesy Phyllis Post.)

There is no question who is a hero in this boy's eyes. This unidentified duo display their patriotism "navy style" in front of their Beech Avenue home in 1954. (Courtesy Brenda Kulp.)

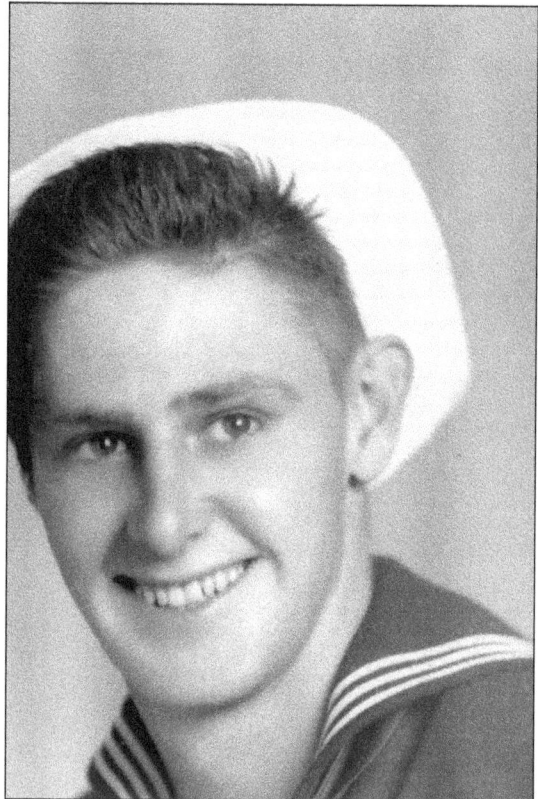

This young hero smiles as he prepares to serve his country. (Courtesy Brenda Kulp.)

Trained, ready, willing, and able, this unidentified young sailor exudes confidence. (Courtesy Brenda Kulp.)

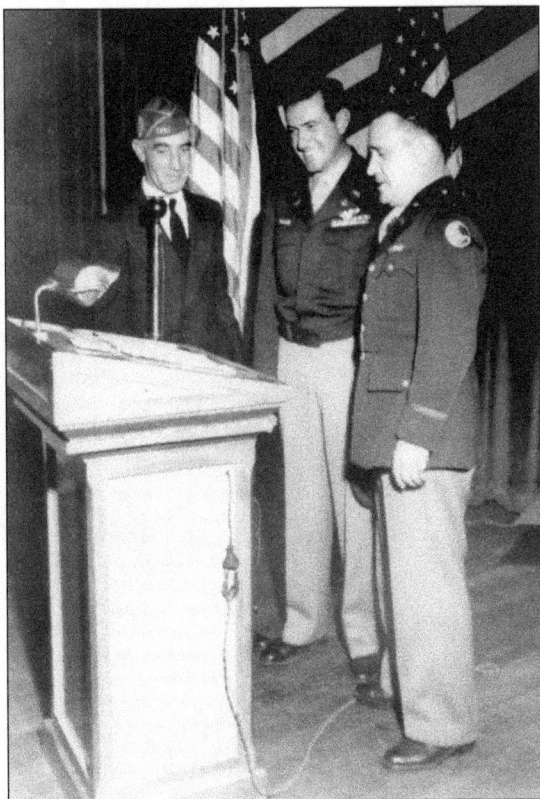

Capt. Louis Zamperini transcended athletic hero status to become a war hero. Here Zamperini, center, steps up to the microphone to address the audience at an American Legion function. His former Boy Scouts of America scoutmaster, Bob Llewellyn (right), proudly stands beside him. (Courtesy Barnard collection.)

Louis Zamperini was in the U.S. Air Force, while his brother Pete chose the U.S. Navy. Both break out the smiles in front of the family car at a neighbor's house on Gramercy Avenue. (Courtesy Barnard collection.)

The Zamperini brothers share grins after being reunited in 1945. (Courtesy Barnard collection.)

Serving her country from the home front, Lois Virginia Scott received the Minute Man war bond banner award with a "T" for Torrance on behalf of the Southern California Gas Company (SCGC). The emblem represented the efforts of more than 90 percent of SCGC employees supporting the United States war effort through the donation of at least 10 percent of their combined wages to purchase war bonds. Flanking her are SCGC officials C. H. Ray, left, and Frank Weiss. Mrs. Scott work in the front office. (Courtesy Gail Scott Kaopua.)

Welcome home! With the war in the Pacific Theater ended, many a tearful reunion occurred in Torrance after V-J Day. This was an especially touching moment for Louis Zamperini, who endured the tremendous double ordeal of being lost at sea and then captured by the Japanese to spend two and a half years as a prisoner. His family was issued the dreaded telegram notifying them of Louie's death. But it wasn't true. Tearful sisters watched in 1945 as their mother, Louise, and Louis, who just arrived home, embraced. Pictured, from left to right, are Virginia, Sylvia, unidentified, unidentified, Louise, and Louis. (Courtesy Barnard collection.)

Standing in front of her home, Virginia Zamperini demonstrates to the neighborhood her love for her country. (Courtesy Barnard collection.)

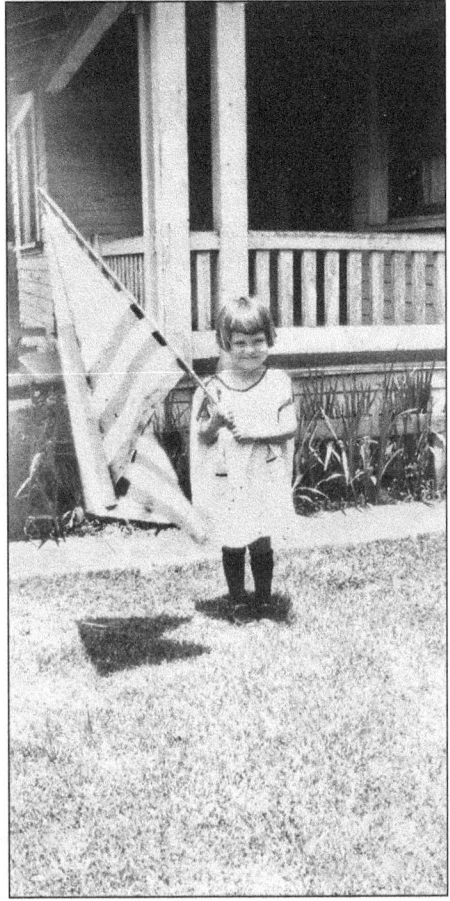

The Zamperini house, located at 2028 Gramercy Avenue, was one of the first 50 homes built for the Dominguez Land Company in 1912. Mrs. Zamperini's brother, Low Dossi of New York, with hat in hand, is the greeter here in the 1930s. Louis Zamperini sits on the porch reading the newspaper. (Courtesy Barnard collection.)

Mr. and Mrs. Anthony Zamperini moved their children from New York to 2028 Gramercy Avenue, Torrance, California. They were so pleased with their new home and community that they invited relatives to come take a look. In the 1920s, they gathered on the porch and the front lawn. Seated in front, from left to right, are Anthony (Tony) and Virginia. Standing directly behind Anthony is Louise Zamperini. (Courtesy Barnard collection.)

The happy couple smiling in front of the corner of their home on Gramercy Avenue is Tony and Louise Zamperini. The Zamperinis epitomized Torrance living—a comfortable home in the beautiful Southern California climate. (Courtesy Barnard collection.)

With a home and family come the necessary chores to keep a household running smoothly, as evidenced by Louise Zamperini preparing to wash dishes. Note the drawer pulls and cabinet latches. (Courtesy Barnard collection.)

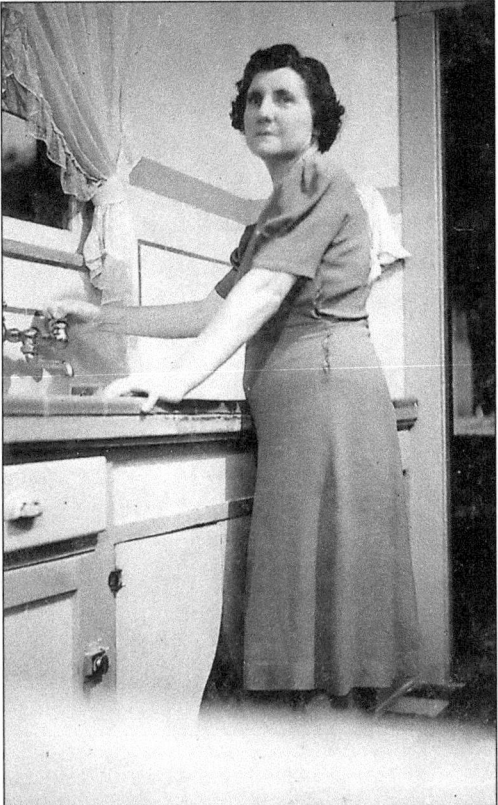

At home, dishes can also be a family effort. In this case, cowboy supervision was apparently necessary in Old Torrance. The metal step-stool chair upon which buckaroo David Scott is seated was a standard item in most homes of the 1950s. With him are Laura Scott, left, and Gail Scott. (Courtesy Gail Scott Kaopua.)

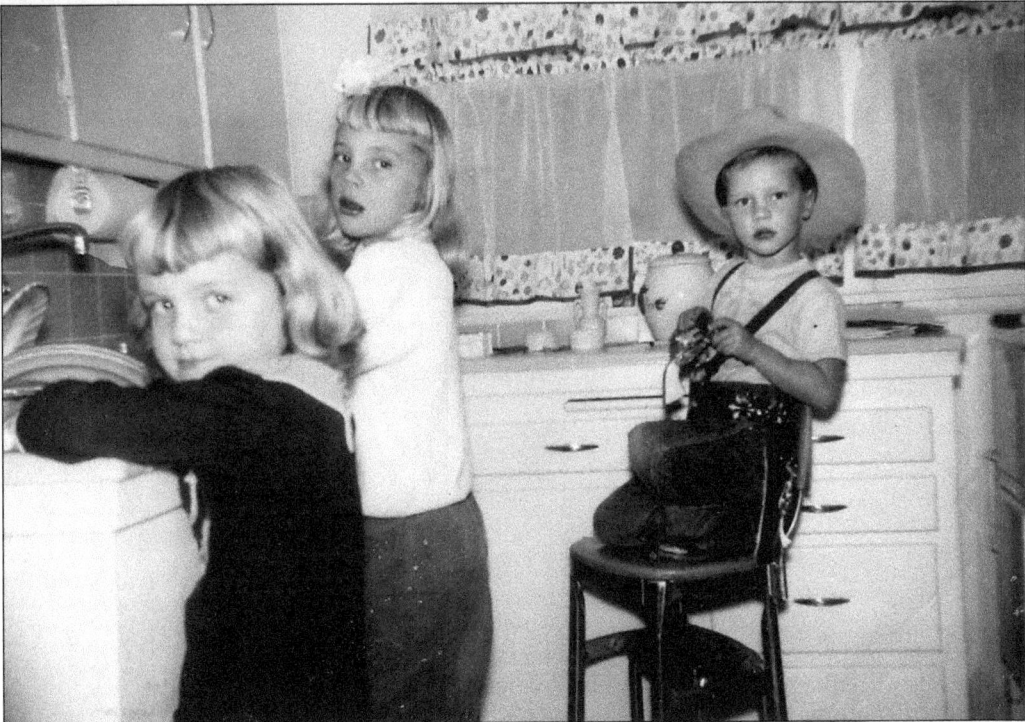

With newspaper bags draped over his body, Bobby Hammond is shown bicycling away from his home on Beech Avenue to deliver the local newspaper to residents. On Sundays, when the paper was larger, his mother, Alice Hammond, helped him get the paper delivered to households around Old Torrance. (Courtesy Alice Burger Hammond.)

At her home on Cedar Avenue, now Crenshaw Boulevard, Alice Burger smiles as she shows off her new dress. (Courtesy Alice Burger Hammond.)

Home life in the city of Torrance, for many youngsters, meant having a dog. On the curb near her home, Jean Burger played with her Chow. (Courtesy Alice Burger Hammond.)

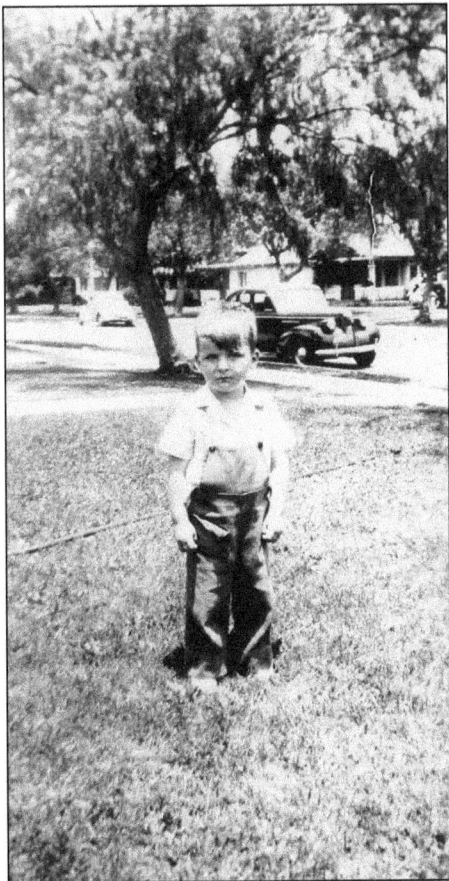

For little Donald Guyan, being at home meant being outside in the grass. Standing in the front yard of 2119 Gramercy Avenue in 1945, he is pictured with a neighbor's car and the growing trees that were planted in Torrance to fulfill the Olmsted vision of a community in harmony with nature. (Courtesy Sara and Ellen Guyan.)

At home in front of his house on Portola Avenue, Mr. Kulp proudly holds his baby daughter Brenda for all to see. Notice the large molding around the door and windows, a feature of the California Craftsman-style homes. (Courtesy Brenda Kulp collection.)

Dogs and kids played an important part in home life. At 2119 Gramercy Avenue are young Donald Guyan and a neighborhood friend playing with a dog on the porch steps. (Courtesy Sara and Ellen Guyan.)

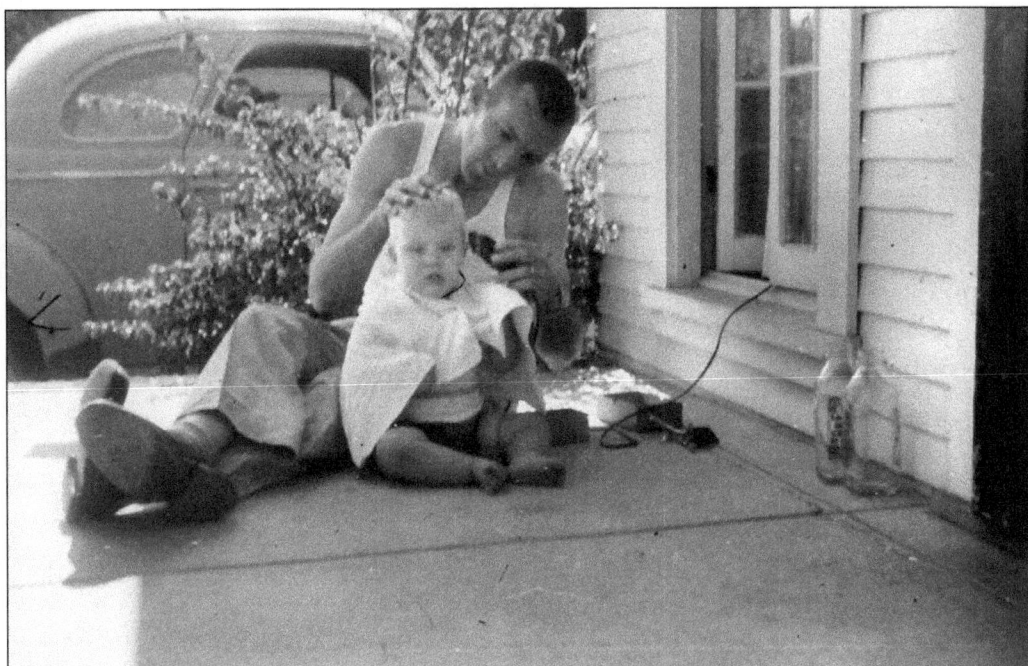

The front porch had a lot of uses, including being a good spot for this 1945 haircut. Bert Scott learned to cut hair in the U.S. Army Air Force during World War II. Here he utilized that skill on young David Scott. On the porch are two glass milk bottles awaiting a new delivery from Hal Hudson's dairy. (Courtesy Gail Scott Kaopua.)

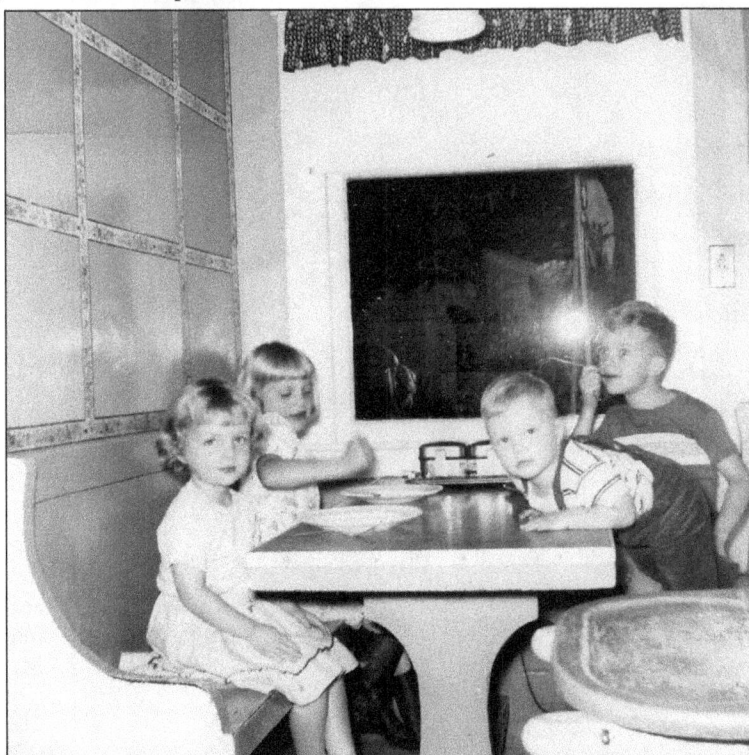

These Scott children didn't need any prodding to exercise their distinct personalities at the kitchen table. Seated, from left to right, are Laura, Gail, Rick, and David, and if the camera doesn't lie, Little Miss Innocence, Demanding Dame, the Family Clown, and "Don't-Forget-Me" Baby respectively. Built-in breakfast nooks like this one were a common feature of the homes built in the city. (Courtesy Gail Scott Kaopua.)

These two share a sisterly bond and practically identical dresses, with vertically striped bodices and horizontally striped flared skirts. These are the Scott girls, Gail, left, and Laura, in 1956. (Courtesy Gail Scott Kaopua.)

Phyllis and George Post happily show off their new baby daughter Peggy at the home of Peggy's maternal grandparents, Mr. and Mrs. McVicar. The home is located at 2120 Gramercy Avenue. (Courtesy Phyllis Post.)

In 1949, Phyllis McVicar Post and her husband, George, celebrate their first Christmas at Phyllis's parent's house, located at 2120 Gramercy Avenue. Pictured, from left to right, are Jack McVicar, Blanche McVicar, Phyllis Post, and George Post. (Courtesy Phyllis Post.)

Another proud mother, Virginia Jones, holds up her daughter Alison in their front yard on Martina Avenue. A lesser family treasure, the convertible, is also seen in this 1949 photograph. (Courtesy Alison Jones.)

In the living room of their home on Marcelina Avenue, these children are ready to leave their fireplace and built-in bookshelves for a trip. The true story is that their mother, Lois Virginia Scott, posed this photograph because she thought the children would look so cute. They were not *really* going anywhere. (Courtesy Gail Scott Kaopua.)

Preparation for Christmas was always a shared family effort. As the two older children decorate the tree and clean up, the younger child sings and gets comfortable. Pictured, from left to right, are the Scott siblings of Old Torrance—Laura, Gail, and Rick. (Courtesy Gail Scott Kaopua collection.)

Mom took this family Christmas photograph with the tree draped in popcorn the family popped and strung with tinsel, which is used to represent icicles. The Scotts, from left to right, are Rick, David, Bert (dad), Gail, and Laura. (Courtesy Gail Scott Kaopua.)

Pianos were an important part of many Torrance families, including the Scotts. However, not all children are happy about playing the piano as noted by the expression of the young girl in the foreground of the photograph. Pictured here, from left to right, are Gail, Rick, Laura, and David. (Courtesy Gail Scott Kaopua.)

Evenings at home often meant telling stories or singing songs. Notice that this family is gathered together away from the new family commodity—the television. Uncle Bud purchased the large box with the little screen for the Scott family. Before this gift, no one in the family had ever seen a television. (Courtesy Gail Scott Kaopua.)

# Six

# THE RESIDENTIAL DISTRICT
## SCHOOL AND FRIENDS

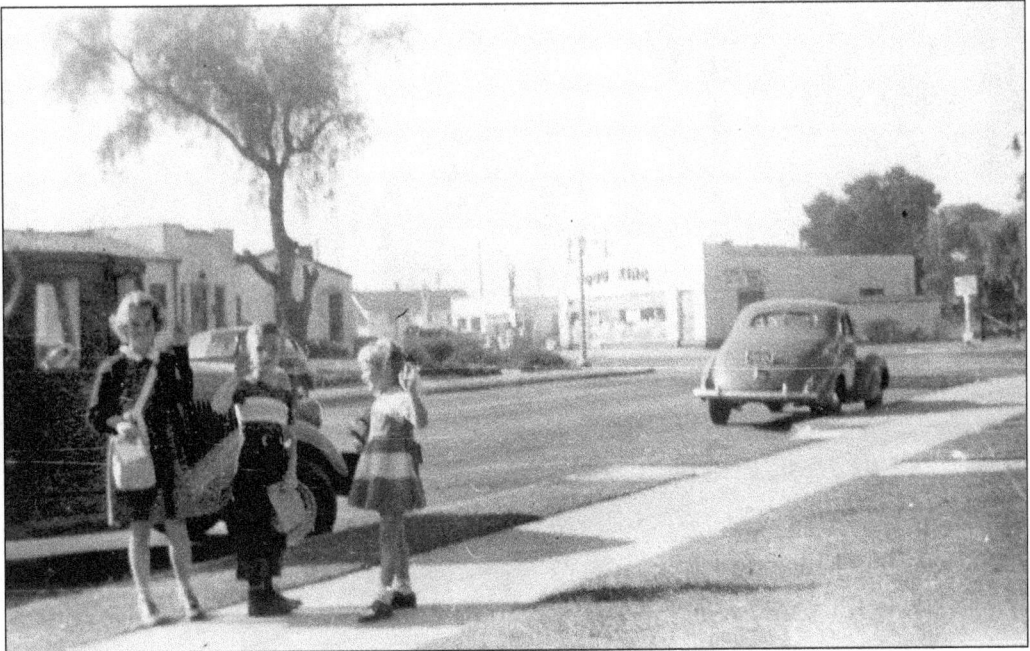

In the 1940s, these Old Torrance neighborhood children carry sack lunches and books on their way to school. Across the street from them are two Spanish-style bungalows. The kids, from left to right, are Joanne Carr, Rick Scott, and Gail Scott. (Courtesy Gail Scott Kaopua.)

This class of pre-kindergartners has completed the "Progress Program" in which they not only utilized both large and small motor skills, but learned the basics to ensure their success in school. In the fourth row is Bobby Hammond. (Courtesy Alice Burger Hammond.)

Although none of the children are identified, this 1950s kindergarten class demonstrates the diversity of its personalities, already forming on the children's faces. Notice the oil derricks in the distance. (Courtesy Alison Jones.)

In the 1950s, Torrance Elementary School was still housed on the same site as Torrance High School. This second grade class posed on the steps of what is today the Home Economics building of Torrance High School. The children's teacher, Miss Lamb, is in the second row, far right. (Courtesy Sara and Ellen Guyan.)

This Torrance Elementary class is about to begin their Christmas vacation. Behind the children is strung the red and green paper chains they made and used to decorate the room. (Courtesy Sara and Ellen Guyan.)

This group of friends is dressed for their eighth-grade graduation. Pictured, from left to right, are Caroline Cunningham, Richard Muranaka, and Alison Jones. (Courtesy Alison Jones.)

−Torrance High School, Torrance, Calif.

Built in 1917 and seen here during the 1920s, Torrance High School was designed by architect Robert Allen Farrel. It sits on the most elevated land in the original City of Torrance. From this point, the pastoral view of El Prado can be seen. (Courtesy Doris Greene.)

This view of Torrance High School has been seen by millions of people—as Beverly Hills High School on the television program *Beverly Hills 90210*. That popularity is one thing, but another prestige significant to the community is that this historic treasure is listed on the National Register of Historic Places. The beautiful structure still serves the teens of the community.

This side view of the auditorium of Torrance High School in 1932 reveals the Mission-style feel of the auditorium.

A closer view shows the entrance to the auditorium and the colonnade. The auditorium was so severely damaged by the 1933 Long Beach earthquake that, although the exterior appeared to be intact, the building had to razed.

The colonnade on the southwest side of the main building of Torrance High School creates a beautiful overhang for students to walk under and still be able to view the campus. The science building is depicted here, behind the colonnade. (Courtesy Alice Burger Hammond.)

Patio High School
Torrance Calif.

H ♥ H

Both of these views of the patio are familiar to millions of viewers of *Beverly Hills 90210* and the early seasons of *Buffy, The Vampire Slayer*, both popular network television programs that were filmed at Torrance High School. (Right Courtesy Alice Burger Hammond.)

Step inside the colonnade to get a feel of what it is like attending school at this historic site. Every student should be so fortunate. (Courtesy Alice Burger Hammond.)

This beautifully adorned 1930 Torrance High School graduating class appears to be very proud of its achievement. They are standing inside the Torrance High School Auditorium. In the first row, fifth from the left, is Louise Hansen, and to the far right is Albert Isen. (Courtesy Fred Hansen Jr.)

In 1934, Bill, Alice, and Kenny enjoy graduation day at Torrance High School. What did their futures hold? Bill attended the University of Hawaii. Alice graduated from the University of Southern California and served as a counselor at her alma mater, Torrance High School, for many years. Kenny Haslem married Alice's sister Jean. (Courtesy Alice Burger Hammond.)

# Torrance High School
## Los Angeles City High School District

his Diploma is awarded to    John W. Guyan
who has been found worthy in Character and Citizenship and
has satisfactorily completed a Course of Study as prescribed
by the Board of Education

Given at Los Angeles, California this    fourth    day of
February nineteen hundred and thirty-eight

Principal

President Board of Education

In 1938, John W. Guyan of Gramercy Avenue graduated from Torrance High School. As his diploma shows, Torrance High School was still a part of the Los Angeles City High School District. (Courtesy Sara and Ellen Guyan.)

Following in the tradition of his father, William (Billy) Guyan graduated from Torrance High School. In this 1961 photograph, he proudly displays his cap and gown in front of the family home at 2119 Gramercy Avenue. The intersection seen here is Gramercy Avenue and 222nd Street. Each of the charming houses can still be seen today. (Courtesy Sara and Ellen Guyan.)

Friendships are made and treasured in Torrance. Here these unidentified "backyard buddies" stop for a photographer. (Courtesy Brenda Kulp.)

Many times, one's best friend is actually related, as in the case of these two friends and sisters, Alice, left, and Jean Burger. (Courtesy Alice Burger Hammond.)

These best friends, Bobby Hammond and his brother Randy Hammond, enjoy their time together. (Courtesy Alice Burger Hammond.)

These Torrance friends, wearing identical dresses, share a bond of friendship. They are Alice Burger, left, and Joy Fossum. (Courtesy Alice Burger Hammond.)

These friends are having fun together at the Torrance Beach. Notice the flattering and modest 1932 swimsuits on Alice Burger, left, and Joy Fossum. This same shot appeared in *Torch*, the Torrance High School yearbook. (Courtesy Alice Burger Hammond.)

These two friends—Marlene Sellfors, left, and Alison Jones—are going to church. In the background on the right is Rick Scott's Woodie. (Courtesy Alison Jones.)

A station wagon and the California Craftsman bungalows on Gramercy Avenue can be seen in the background, as Billy Guyan chats with a neighbor. (Courtesy Sara and Ellen Guyan.)

One can't help but smile back at these best friends from Beech Avenue. These four-year-old friends spent a lot of time playing at one another's home. Bobby Hammond is on the right. (Courtesy Alice Burger Hammond.)

These high school friends and sweethearts stand arm in arm in a front yard on Cedar Avenue They are, from left, Bill Beckert, Alice Burger, Jean Burger, and Kenneth Haslen. (Courtesy Alice Burger Hammond.)

In 1934, these friends and sweethearts spend a romantic afternoon under the tree. A neighbor's car is parked in the street. (Courtesy Alice Burger Hammond.)

This unidentified group of girls constitutes the neighbors and friends who lived on Amapola Avenue. (Courtesy Brenda Kulp.)

This unidentified little darling performs for her family in Old Torrance, c. 1939. (Courtesy Brenda Kulp.)

In 1944, these munchkins, John Guyan, left, and Donald Guyan, in cuffed pants and suspenders, are playing at Torrance Beach. Behind them are many of the townspeople's automobiles. (Courtesy Sara and Ellen Guyan.)

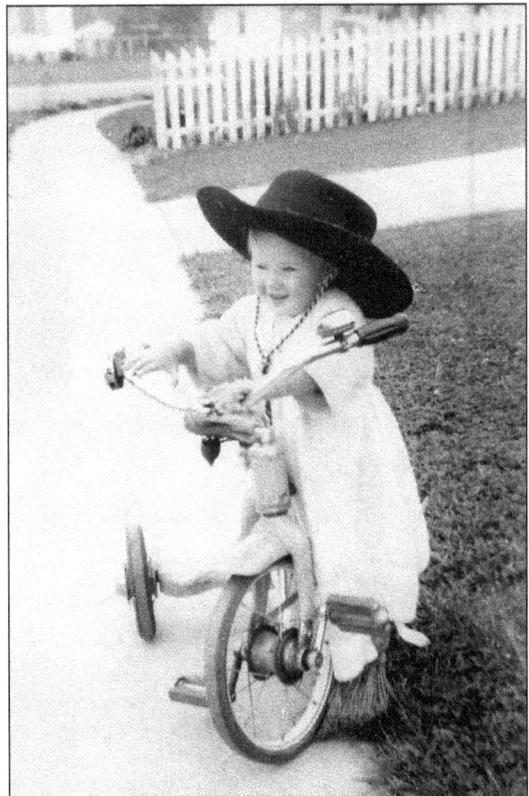

This little cowgirl thinks she is going to ride big brother's tricycle, even though that is an impossibility. She seems happy just trying. The tricycle was a gift to her big brother Gordie after he had the measles and the doctor recommended he stay inside away from light. To coax Gordie to follow the doctor's order, his parents, Gordon and Virginia Jones, promised him this tricycle. Nevertheless, it is little Alison who thinks it is hers. (Courtesy Alison Jones.)

It is not difficult to be the only girl in this group of Amapola neighborhood kids playing. The "Tricycle Brigade" rides. (Courtesy Brenda Kulp.)

Hats and tricycles were all that were needed for these two boys in 1943. Bobby Church, left, grinned as he balanced his too big sombrero and peddled his tricycle. His pal, John A. Guyan, wears a sweater hat. All of the houses seen in the background still sit on Gramercy Avenue. (Courtesy Sara and Ellen Guyan.)

Pushing and pulling on this four-wheeled pull cart that seated two was part of the fun for these two neighborhood buddies, John A. Guyan and Bobby Church. Tricycles were a form of play for little kids and older kids alike. On the tricycle in 1945 is Donald Guyan. (Courtesy Sara and Ellen Guyan.)

At play in the front yard of their Gramercy Avenue house are the two Guyan brothers—Donald, on the tricycle, and John. (Courtesy Sara and Ellen Guyan.)

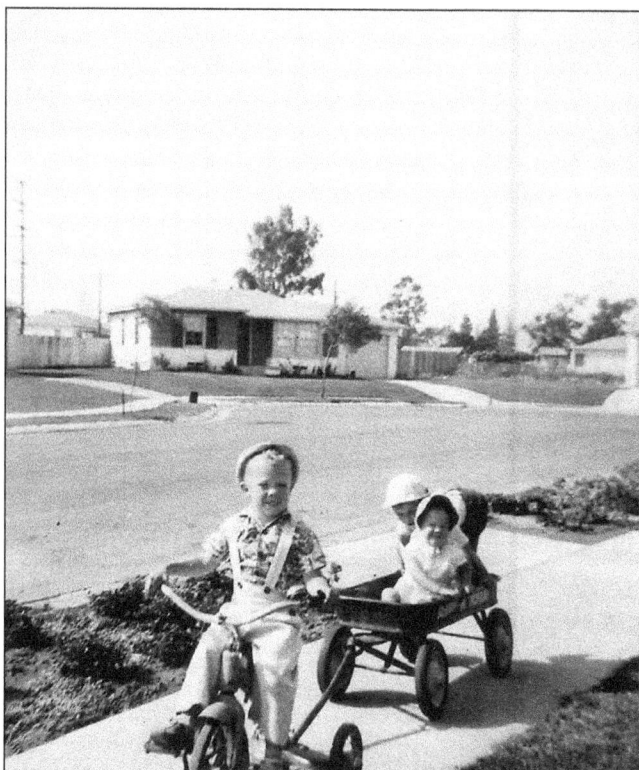

Playing sometimes means a real workout for the legs. Little Gordie Jones, all recovered from the measles, proudly rode his tricycle and pulled his little sister Alison and a friend in the Radio Flyer. (Courtesy Alison Jones.)

Playing for this unidentified little girl meant a ride for her and her puppy on big brother's bicycle. The puppy, Jiggs, rode in the bag behind the seat. (Look by the young man's leg to see the puppy.) Yes, that's a cigar in his mouth—people didn't know better in those days. The house in the background is on Sierra Place. (Courtesy Brenda Kulp.)

Playing with the hose was apparently this youngster's pastime. What better way to stay cool and water the lawn at the same time? Notice the barn-style roofline of the house. Several of these can still be seen in the Residential District. (Courtesy Brenda Kulp.)

Gathering together and playing in the front yard was a common experience for these neighborhood children on Marcelina Avenue. In the background, notice the mature trees and the large open porches of the Craftsman bungalows. The kids, from left to right, are (first row) Laura Scott, with the teddy bear, and Gail Scott; (second row) Rick Scott and Joanne Carr. (Courtesy Gail Scott Kaopua.)

Rick Scott, in cuffed pants and tucked-in Torrance Elementary School T-shirt, demonstrates that he is finished with his raking and ready for play—pulling his younger brother David in his Radio Special. Behind Rick and David are the decorative corbels that support the roof, as well as pairs of 10-light windows on each side of the door. (Courtesy Gail Scott Kaopua.)

Another group of neighbors spent their afternoons together playing attired in the threads of the era—girls in dresses and boys in cowboy shirts. (Courtesy Gail Scott Kaopua.)

Play isn't only for kids. This little puppy, known as Blackie, wanted to join in as this sailor, Bobby Hammond, clutches a Raggedy Ann doll. (Courtesy Alice Burger Hammond.)

Playing the "Wild West" on Beech Avenue, this cowgirl and cowboy have everything they need—the cowgirl, with not only her hat and gun, but also her scarf and gloves, and the cowboy his hat and rifle. The cowgirl's last name was Ritchie, and Bobby Hammond is on the right. (Courtesy Alice Burger Hammond.)

Adults have their own form of play. This pilot, home from the war, enjoys listening to long-playing records in the living room with his sisters. Pictured, from left to right, are Louis Zamperini, Virginia Zamperini, and Sylvia Zamperini Flammer. (Courtesy Barnard collection.)

The cowboy and cowgirl are ready for the swing set in the backyard. The Ritchie girl is again seen with Bobby Hammond. (Courtesy Alice Burger Hammond.)

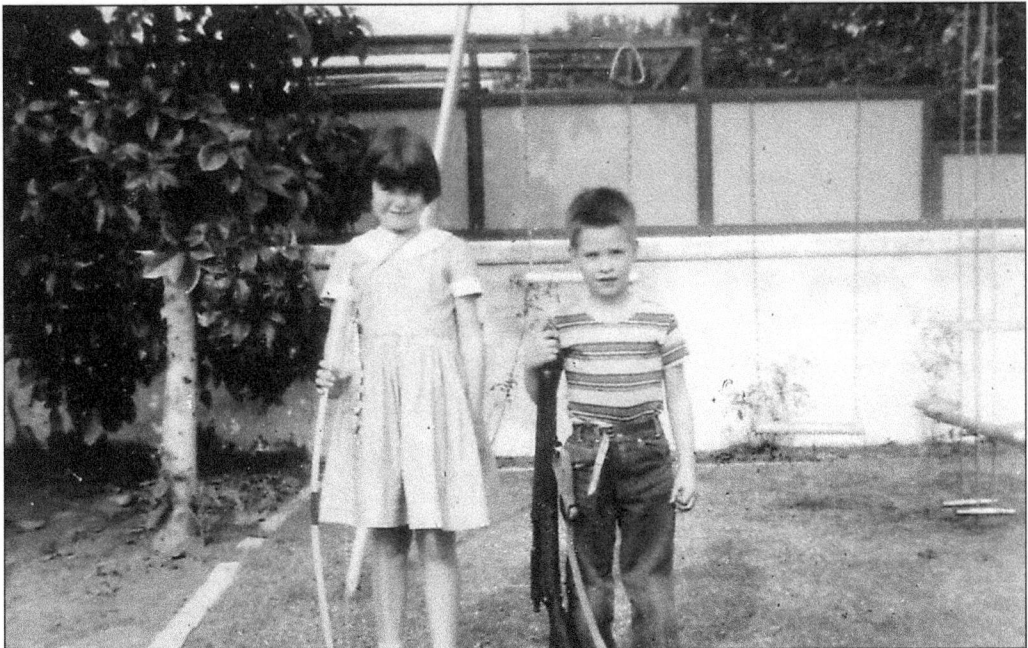

The backyard action was joined by more neighborhood kids. This unidentified duo has just finished playing cowboy and Indian with a bow and arrow and rifle. (Courtesy Alice Burger Hammond.)

Another play day involved this Jim Dandy kite that father and son—Bob and Bobby Hammond—are attempting to put into flight. Bob Hammond is untangling the tail, while young Bobby holds the string. Both father and son have almost the same expression of intense concentration as they work to prepare the kite for another attempt at flight. (Courtesy Alice Burger Hammond.)

The Jim Dandy is airborne! Bob Hammond worked to keep it up, as Bobby's face clearly showed his delight at this experience. The kite's tail can be seen to the right of Bobby. (Courtesy Alice Burger Hammond.)

Typical of childhood ingenuity, Mike Medved took the large packing box and, with a little work, created his own playhouse—a most inexpensive toy for any little boy's play day. (Courtesy Alice Burger Hammond.)

This big oak tree has lost its autumn leaves, but it still brings a sense of contentment to climb and sit in it. The tree, on Beech Avenue, was used by just about every child in the neighborhood. It had one especially large branch that grew almost to the corner of the block and that branch provided a great lookout. (Courtesy Alice Burger Hammond.).

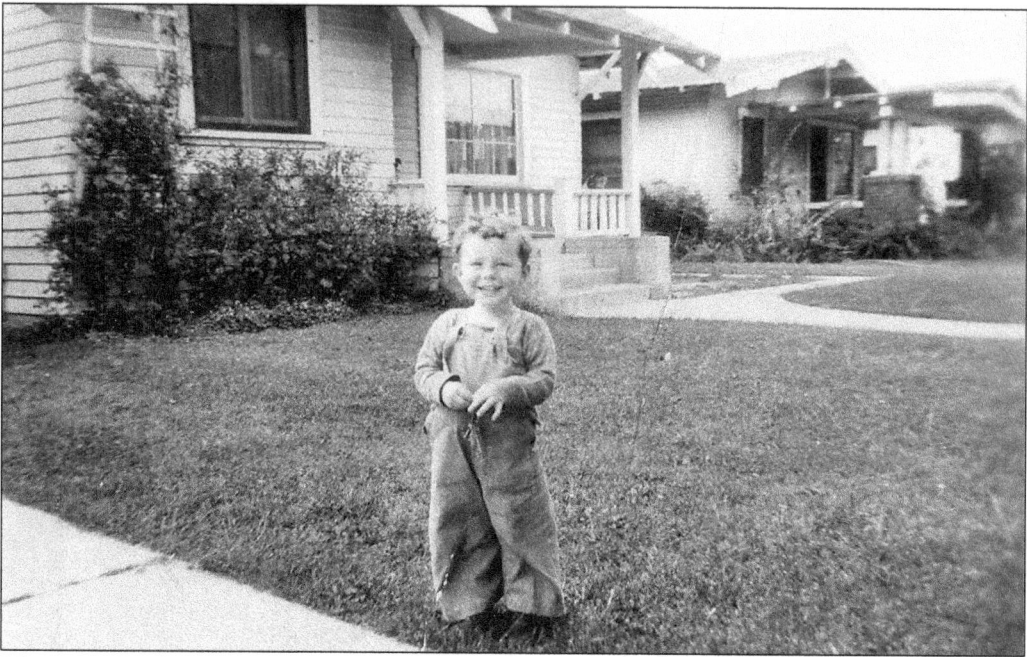

This overalls-clad lad is "Giggles," or John A. Guyan. Behind him are, from left to right, 2119, 2117, and 2115 Gramercy Avenue. (Courtesy Sara and Ellen Guyan.)

Playing at Easter time involved what else? An Easter Egg Hunt! This group clearly enjoyed the hunt and proudly display the eggs they found. Alison and Gordie Jones are among the kids. (Courtesy Alison Jones.)

Of course, play also meant dress-up, as evidenced by "Shirley Temple." (Courtesy Gail Scott Kaopua.)

The Hammond cousins are seen in the backyard. Notice the modest swimsuits and cuffed jeans, as well as the little boy's reinforced knees. Among the kids, second and third from left, are Bobby and Steven Randal. (Courtesy Alice Burger Hammond collection.)

Another group of unidentified neighbors are at play in the backyard. This time, they enjoy the Dough Boy pool. Note the mature tree that graces both backyards. (Courtesy Gail Scott Kaopua collection.)

At the Victor E. Benstead Plunge, kids practice aquatic performances, swim laps, boat, dive, and enjoy the sunshine and water. (Courtesy Doris Greene.)

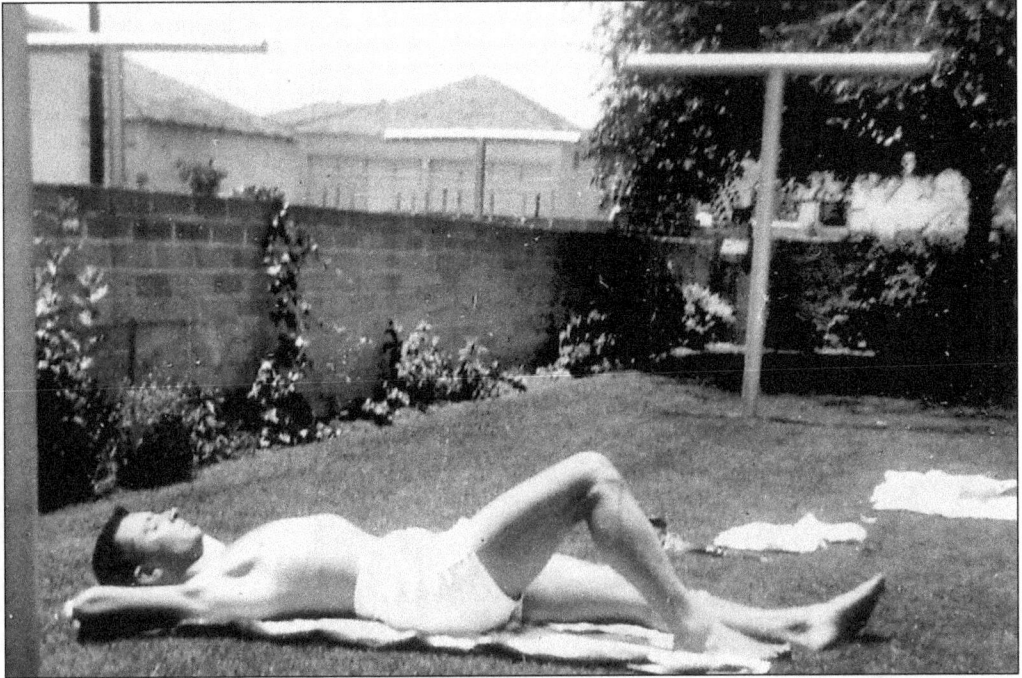

Some adults choose a less crowded place to play. For Bob Hammond, that meant relaxing and sunbathing in his own backyard on Beech Street. (Courtesy Alice Burger Hammond.)

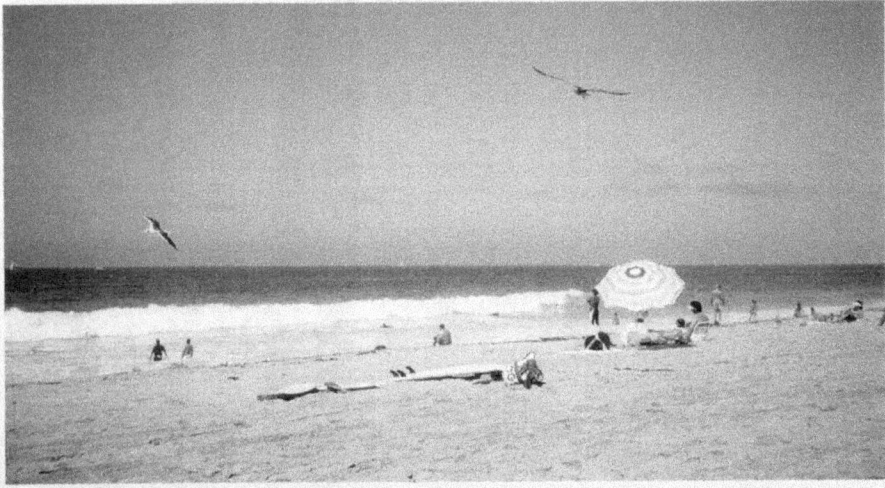

Although it is located outside of the original city designed by Olmsted, the Torrance Beach, once annexed by the city, became a welcomed place for Torrance residents to play. (Courtesy Doris Greene.)

Gordie Jones, left, and Bill Wasenburg, load up the Woodie with boards and friends before heading to the beach. Gordie purchased the Woodie, an ambulance car during World War II, with new tires and a full tank of gasoline for $100. (Courtesy Alison Jones collection.)

After a day of surfing, Bill Wasenburg pokes his head above Bob Duery, while Gordie Jones grins beside his board. (Courtesy Alison Jones.)

Torrance Park, seen here in the 1950s, still provides a great place for a family barbeque or picnic, and a great play area for children. About to head to the play area are five-year-old Laura Scott and three-year-old David Scott. (Courtesy Gail Scott Kaopua.)

Doing exactly what both Jared S. Torrance and Frederick Law Olmsted Jr. envisioned, these mothers and their children are enjoying the excellent climate and the beautifully landscaped open space at Torrance Park. (Courtesy University of Southern California Regional History collection.)

-LOOK FOR THE GOLDEN ARCHES® McDonald's

This McDonald's postcard was sent to Torrance residents to provide ideas for playtime. It advertised to "Present this card for a free 100% pure beef hamburger and a serving of crisp golden French fries at 1452 W. Carson St. This is our way of acquainting you with the tastiest food in town and the real pleasure of eating at McDonald's. Come in any time—bring your family and enjoy food and service as you like it! McDonald's makes everything so good, inviting and convenient too. Look for the Golden Arches where quality starts fresh every day." (Courtesy Doris Greene.)

The Scott children— Gail, David, and Laura—are ready to go trick-or-treating in the neighborhood dressed as a clown, a hobo, and a Roaring Twenties girl. All the costumes were made with things found at home. (Courtesy Gail Scott Kaopua.)

The Jones family, with the camper hitched to a 1953 Pontiac, is about to leave on a camping trip. (Courtesy Alison Jones.)

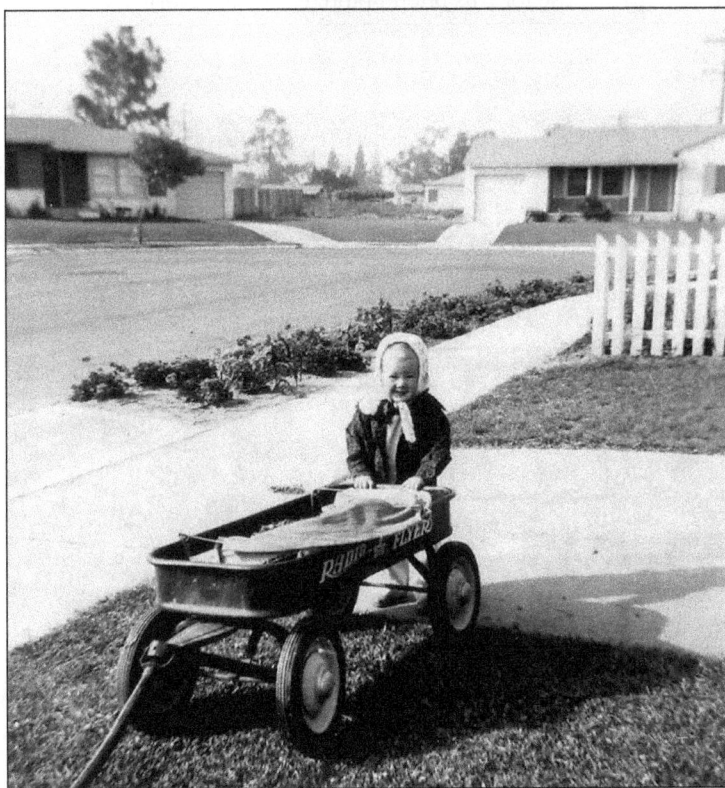

This little one attempts to push the Radio Flyer, knowing that the wagon is suppose to go, just not sure how. (Courtesy Alison Jones.)

In 1920, this dressed-up group obviously enjoyed a great party at the Murray Hotel. They took a break from the festivities long enough to pose for this photograph. (Courtesy Doris Greene.)

In 1956, inside the Torrance High School Auditorium, the band, flag squad, and majorettes devote their playtime to practice and excellence. Donald Guyan is in the second row. (Courtesy Sara and Ellen Guyan.)

## HOLLYWOOD U.S.O.
### EVENTS OF THE WEEK

Location — 1531 N. Cahuenga Blvd. — One-half Block North of Sunset — Hollywood, California

MERLE WATERMAN, Director    JIM SEXTON, Chief of Staff    HARRY MYNATT, Associate    REXFORD BELLAMY, Program Director

Week of October 2nd....to....October 8th, 1944

# Friendship House
## for Servicemen
## and Servicewomen

That's the way the many hundreds of volunteer hostesses and hosts and the staff of the Hollywood U.S.O. want all you GI Joe's and Jane's to feel about this big place of ours. Remember it is your place. Our doors are open from 9 to 11 every day— all night Saturday. Entertainment—dancing—every night—FREE "eats" day & night.

"Lady Trilby"
S.D. Wilcox-Owner & Trainer

## Party Nights

Clubs of Hollywood & Los Angeles are Your special hosts
See them here

1. Rose Marie Wenger  2. Dick Love  3. Dorothy Ertel

**Monday**

**Tuesday**

**Wednesday**

Torranceonians not only play, but also provide service. This flyer was posted in the local military camps to notify the enlisted men that there was entertainment for them. This particular flyer details a variety of performances, including one to be held at Torrance High School. (Courtesy Sara and Ellen Guyan.)

In 1944, Torrance High students proudly participated in raising funds for the USO during World War II by hosting a production of the *Kentucky Mountaineers*. Here John R. Guyan performs as a full house looks on. Check the expressions in the audience; Torrance has been a great place to play, in many ways.

On stage, John R. Guyan and his leading actress, Bea Carrick, perform *Kentucky Mountaineers* for a delighted crowd. (Courtesy Sara and Ellen Guyan.)

In 1955, these young women served in the Rotary Club and were known as the "Rotary Anns." Pictured, from left to right, are Marian Ensigner, Jane Myers, Audry Marcee, and Phyllis Post. (Courtesy Phyllis Post.)

At Torrance Beach, these Torrance Jaycees Juniors are pictured making ice cream with rock salt and ice cream makers that had to be hand-cranked. (Courtesy Fred Hansen Jr.)

These Torrance spectators show their appreciation at a local sports event. In the second row are Pete and Louis Zamperini. (Courtesy Barnard collection.)

These men, all employees of the National Supply Company, belonged to the same Moose Lodge. and are all proud winners of the bowling championship. Gordon Jones in the middle. (Courtesy Alison Jones.)

Ready to participate in the Torrance parade to celebrate the city's All America City award, these ladies give a peek at how they intend to stave off the winter chill—long johns under their formal gowns. They rode the Beta Sigma Phi float in the mile-long celebration parade on January 26, 1957, while 15,000 Torranceonians looked on. Pictured here, from left to right, are Dorothy Hadler, Grace Lynch, Priscilla Swisher, and Pat Wolfe.

"Play" for many of the local adults meant an evening of cocktails, good food, and good friends at The Palms Restaurant on Carson Street. The Palms was the social gathering place enjoyed by just about every grownup in Old Torrance. (Courtesy Alan Schwartz.)

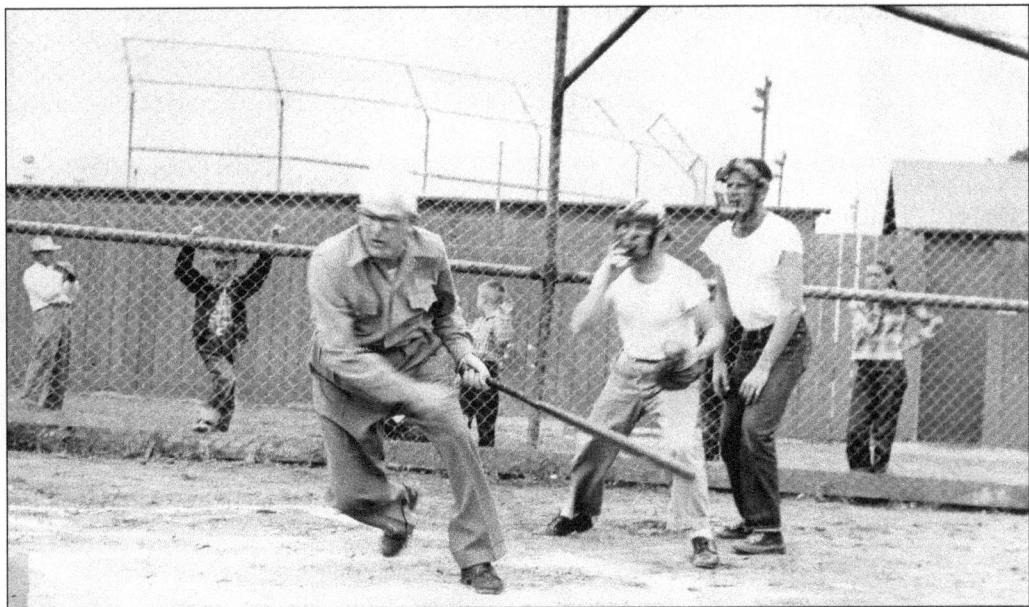

Batting a home run is Sam Levy, who began what would become one of the longest running businesses in Old Torrance. Levy lived out Jared Sidney Torrance's vision of a community in which the citizens are happy to live, to work, and to play. Just being a Torranceonian is a "home run." (Courtesy Alan Schwartz.)

# BIBLIOGRAPHY

Aldershof, Gertrude, et al. *History of Torrance: A Teacher's Resource Guide*. Torrance, CA: Torrance Board of Education, 1964.

Campbell, Thomas D. and Company. *Torrance: The Modern Industrial City*. Los Angeles, CA: Campbell, 1913.

Dalton, Peggy Coleman. *Torrance: A City for Today*. Chatsworth, CA: Windsor Publications Inc., 1990.

Gillingham, Robert Cameron. *The Rancho San Pedro: The Story of the Rancho in Los Angeles County and of Its Owners, the Dominguez Family*. Carson, CA: Dominguez Properties, 1961.

Grenier, Judson A., and Robert Cameron Gillingham. *California Legacy: The James Alexander Watson-Marie Dolores Dominguez de Watson Family, 1820–1980*. Carson, CA: Watson Land Company, 1987.

Hines, Thomas S. *Irving Gill and the Architecture of Reform: A Study in Modernist Architecture*. New York: Monacelli Press, 2000.

Kamerling, Bruce. *Irving J. Gill, Architect*. San Diego, CA: San Diego Historical Society, 1993.

Kielbasa, John R. *Historic Adobes of Los Angeles County*. Pittsburgh, PA: Dorrance Publishing Co. Inc., 1997.

Klaus, Susan L. *A Modern Arcadia*. Frederick Law Olmsted Jr. and the Plan for Forest Hills Garden. Boston, MA: University of Massachusettes Press, 2002.

Mason, William M. *Early Dominguez Families and Settlement of the Rancho San Pedro*. Carson, CA: California State University, Dominguez Hills, 1991.

"Olmsted, Frederick Law Jr." *Current Biography*, June 1949

Olmsted, James F. *The Story of Torrance*. McLean, VA: James F. Olmsted, 1992.

Shanahan, Dennis F., and Charles Elliott Jr. *Historic Torrance: A Pictorial History of Torrance, California*. Redondo Beach, CA: Legends Press, 1984.

Stevenson, Elizabeth. *Park Maker: A Life of Frederick Law Olmsted* [Sr.]. New York: Macmillan Publishing Co., 1977.

Torrance, Jared Sidney. *The Decendants of Lewis Hart and Anne Elliott*. South Pasadena: Mrs. Jared Sidney Torrance, 1923.

Visit us at
arcadiapublishing.com

www.ingramcontent.com/pod-product-compliance
Lightning Source LLC
Chambersburg PA
CBHW050711110426
42813CB00007B/2150